# Best Practices in Grant Seeking
## Beyond the Proposal

Saadia Faruqi

Edited By
P. D. Esmeralda Valague

**JONES AND BARTLETT PUBLISHERS**
*Sudbury, Massachusetts*
BOSTON      TORONTO      LONDON      SINGAPORE

*World Headquarters*

| Jones and Bartlett Publishers | Jones and Bartlett Publishers | Jones and Bartlett Publishers |
|---|---|---|
| 40 Tall Pine Drive | Canada | International |
| Sudbury, MA 01776 | 6339 Ormindale Way | Barb House, Barb Mews |
| 978-443-5000 | Mississauga, Ontario L5V 1J2 | London W6 7PA |
| info@jbpub.com | Canada | United Kingdom |
| www.jbpub.com | | |

Jones and Bartlett's books and products are available through most bookstores and online booksellers. To contact Jones and Bartlett Publishers directly, call 800-832-0034, fax 978-443-8000, or visit our website, www.jbpub.com.

This publication is designed to provide accurate and authoritative information in regard to the Subject Matter covered. It is sold with the understanding that the publisher is not engaged in rendering legal, accounting, or other professional service. If legal advice or other expert assistance is required, the service of a competent professional person should be sought.

**Production Credits**
Publisher: Michael Brown
Editorial Assistant: Catie Heverling
Editorial Assistant: Teresa Reilly
Senior Production Editor: Tracey Chapman
Senior Marketing Manager: Sophie Fleck
Manufacturing and Inventory Control Supervisor: Amy Bacus
Composition: DSCS/Absolute Service, Inc.
Cover Design: Scott Moden
Cover Image: © Mirko Tabasevic/Dreamstime.com
Printing and Binding: Malloy, Inc.
Cover Printing: Malloy, Inc.

**Library of Congress Cataloging-in-Publication Data**
Faruqi, Saadia.
    Best practices in grant seeking : beyond the proposal / by Saadia Faruqi.
      p. cm.
    Includes bibliographical references and index.
    ISBN-13: 978-0-7637-7487-5 (pbk.)
    ISBN-10: 0-7637-7487-1 (pbk.)
    1. Fund raising—United States. 2. Nonprofit organizations—United States—Finance. 3. Proposal writing for grants—United States—Finance. 4. Fund raising. 5. Nonprofit organizations. 6. Proposal writing for grants. I. Title.
    HG177.5.U6F374 2009
    658.15'224—dc22

                                    2009029415
6048

**Printed in the United States of America**
13 12 11 10 09   10 9 8 7 6 5 4 3 2 1

# Acknowledgments

This book is dedicated to my husband Nasir, and my children Mubashir and Mariam, who endured silently while this book was being researched and written. Thank you.

My gratitude also extends to all those grant writers, development directors, executive directors, and foundation officials who participated in my research, and spent countless hours answering my questions over the phone and via email. Your involvement is a true indication of your passion for grant seeking and your eagerness to benefit the nonprofit community.

# Contents

# About the Author

Saadia Faruqi, president of Faruqi & Associates, has almost 10 years of grant writing and development experience in the nonprofit sector, including at-risk youth, women's health, domestic violence, science education, adult and family literacy, and the arts. She also has extensive experience in public relations, communications, marketing, and finance.

Prior to founding Faruqi & Associates, Saadia worked as Grants Administrator and later Grants Consultant for Big Brothers Big Sisters of Greater Houston. She has also served as Development Director of Literacy Advance of Houston. She holds a Bachelor of Science in Business Administration from the University of Central Florida and a Bachelor of Business Administration from the University of Karachi, in her native country of Pakistan. In 2001, she received the prestigious President's Student Service Award, granted by George W. Bush for volunteerism and student leadership.

Saadia has always focused on improving the nonprofit sector; her research projects include a study on the relationships between funders and grantee organizations and how this impacts the grants awarded. This study, entitled "Grantor-Grantee Relationships—A Research Study" was published in the *Journal of the American Association of Grant Professionals*, Fall/Winter 2004 Issue. Saadia is a member of the American Association of Grant Professionals, and founder and past Chair of the Grant Writers' Network of Greater Houston, an organization dedicated to providing professional development, training, and networking opportunities for grant writers in the Houston area.

Saadia works and lives in Houston, Texas, with her husband and two young children.

# The Call for Grant Seeking Strategies

*"Before we even get to the proposal, my advice is to really know what you are applying for, and who you are applying to, and then to align your request with the mission of the foundation. You can have the best organization or the best program in the world but it won't get funded if you don't do the homework and the research before applying."*

Deena Epstein, Senior Program Officer
George Gund Foundation

Grant writing can be an art or a science, depending on who you ask. The artist chooses each word with the utmost care, weaving stories and vivid descriptions into the proposal, and making sure each finished product is a living, breathing entity capable of inspiring the reader to give. The scientist relies on extensive data and studies to create powerful documents that, once complete, will not be tampered with except to be updated with more current information. The average grant professional lies somewhere in between the two ends of this spectrum. The three types seem like a mixed bunch, were it not for one unifying factor: the grant proposal itself.

As a grants consultant, I find that the majority of my time is spent writing. That is not surprising, since I love to write. In fact, many grant professionals initially enter this profession because it gives them permission to hide behind their computers crafting words and sentences into case statements, proposals, and other written documents. They converse with other grant professionals, but mostly to seek their advice about how to write better; they attend networking sessions, but mainly those that have an educational component such as foundation research or persuasive writing. In their early days, they attend courses and read books that promise to teach them how to create the perfect proposal. After a few years, they may even begin teaching the same techniques to newcomers.

What seems wrong with this picture? Absolutely nothing! I doubt that I would be where I am today without that almost obsessive drive to improve my grant writing skills and share my knowledge with others. But I also learned something valuable along the way, as I navigated the path from newbie to resident grant writer at a large organization, and later consultant to many smaller nonprofits. It is rarely enough to write excellent proposals and sit back, waiting for them to get funded. No matter how brilliant the writer, it is not the proposal that gets accepted—or rejected—but the program and the people who run it. A colleague once remarked that expecting a grant professional to produce grant funding in a vacuum is like asking them to spin gold from straw.

Yet that is exactly what many grant professionals across the country experience almost every day in their jobs. Be they trained writers, consultants, volunteers, or program staff, these hardy individuals bear the burden of supporting a large portion of their organization's budget; their only motivation a rallying cry from their leaders: "let's apply for grants!" At the same time, as the competition for private foundation dollars becomes increasingly more intense, nonprofit organizations are struggling to find competent grant professionals who can show results. Even organizations with multimillion dollar budgets and entire development departments at their disposal are sometimes unsuccessful in raising the funds they need through foundation grants. It would be extremely simplistic, even naïve, to suggest that the person who wrote the grant proposal is to blame.

At the beginning of my career, I often felt guilty if my proposals on behalf of any one organization consistently failed to bring in money. As my experience grew, so did my appreciation of the various factors influencing institutional funding. It took me a while to realize that while my skills and expertise were certainly important, I could not achieve the results I sought unless I had the support of my board, and my organization was conducting ongoing community engagement. My proposals could sing the praises of my agency, but when funders showed up for a tour, reality would raise its head—and it may not be as pretty as my words. In a nutshell, I could be the best writer possible, but it would never be enough without strategies and plans created at the top involving all departments and programs.

During a study of U.S. and Canadian nonprofits in 2004, I learned that organizations typically do not provide sufficient support and involvement to the grant seeking process at the leadership level, leaving grant professionals to be researchers, relationship-builders, community advocates, program designers, reporters, and grant managers (1). Many grant professionals use the training they receive to write cookie cutter proposals and send mass mailings to foundations that "fit the profile." Very few organizations, regardless of size, create grant seeking strategies that include not just the writer, but programs and public relations staff, board members, volunteers, and even clients. This is done in many cases for other fundraising activities, such as major gifts or capital campaigns and even special events, but almost never for grants. Many organizations endeavor to get small grants from multiple foundations for the sake of covering operating costs; others strive for a few big contributions to keep them afloat. There is often a lack of strategic planning when it comes to grant seeking, and grant professionals are expected to work in a vacuum without a deeper understanding of what affects foundation giving and why.

# Research Methodology

This book uses the collective voice of organizations and foundations throughout the United States to bring home the importance of grant seeking strategies. In late 2007, our company embarked upon a nationwide research on 240 nonprofit organizations (200 organizations participated in an online survey and 40 organizations in telephone and in-person interviews), as well as 20 foundations to assess the factors that lead to successful grants. The study utilized a mixed method research methodology that first surveyed nonprofit organizations throughout the country on a number of topics, and then conducted in-depth interviews on the same topics. The factors under investigation were:

- Board and senior staff relationships with foundations
- Site visits by potential funders
- Nonsoliciting contact and stewardship practices
- Public relations efforts by nonprofits
- Experience of grant writers
- Quality of grant proposals
- Quality of programs and outcome measurement
- Collaborative efforts between nonprofits

During an 18-month period, grant writers, development staff, and nonprofit leaders who participated in the research disclosed their challenges and shared best practices. At the same time, foundation officials revealed what was important to them in terms of proposal content, site visits, collaborations, and sustainability. While the grant proposal was discussed, its value was proved to be secondary in most cases. The aim of the research and this subsequent book is to learn from the profiled people and organizations and identify areas where one's own boards and staff can improve.

For the purpose of the research, we categorized nonprofits based on their budget size in order to identify needs and challenges (see Figure A). The category of *small budgets* ($500,000 or less) was created because these are

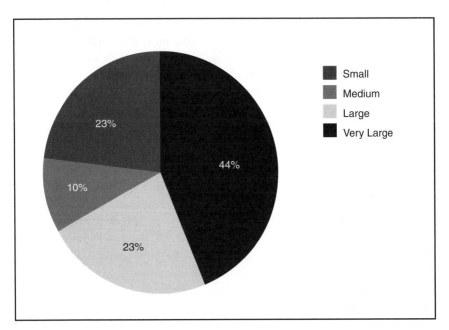

Figure A  *Budget Categories of Respondents*

mostly grassroots organizations with severe budget and expertise constraints that discourage them from adopting grant seeking strategies. Such organizations typically have program boards and a high amount of volunteer involvement, leaving little understanding or ability to approach foundations or to raise funds strategically. The next category is *medium budgets* of $500,000 to $1 million, created because these organizations have typically taken the next step and progressed to more advanced fundraising and programmatic practices and may have the resources for a dedicated development staff person. Public relations efforts of such nonprofits are also somewhat sophisticated.

The third category consists of organizations with *large budgets* between $1–5 million. The differentiation of this type of organization also has a rationale: at this level, most organizations have development staff of more than one person, and grant writers are usually not involved in other development, marketing, or program areas. At this level, nonprofit boards are somewhat fundraising boards, but the attention to grant seeking is still lacking. However, they typically have more sophisticated public relations practices and programwise have attained a high level of expertise. The final category of *very large budgets* (above $5 million) may seem simplistic to some, as many of our respondents—and probably readers of this book as well—belong to organizations with $20–50 million budgets; some may even have budgets of $100 million. The reasoning behind the lumping together of larger organizations is this: above the $5 million level, and certainly beyond that, organizations typically seek a large portion of their funds through government sources, and their individual and major gifts fundraising practices are highly advanced. Therefore, for the purposes of our research (with an emphasis on foundation grants), we felt that it was feasible to categorize them together.

# Results

We discovered through our research that the major factors affecting grant funding include board relationships with funders, positive community image, successful site visits before the grant award, nonsoliciting contact with funders, good reporting practices, and well-designed programs. Intuitively as well as through experience, most grant professionals realize some or all of this on their own; convincing their supervisors and implementing new practices within their organizations is another matter altogether. Hence, the research promises to give proponents of the grant seeking approach a tool to take to decision-makers for added support of their arguments.

Further, the real world examples in this book are valuable for organizations who do believe that change is necessary but are unsure as to how to bring about that change. Rather than lecture about techniques and processes, this book highlights numerous best practices of organizations that have achieved a high level of expertise in the factors under investigation, and gives countless examples of how to bring about small improvements in one's own backyard. Whether the reader belongs to a grassroots agency or a multi-million dollar nonprofit, he or she should be able to adapt some of these best practices and see the results before long. Currently, no other research exists to offer hard evidence of factors affecting foundation funding; therefore, the information provided here is not only invaluable but also cutting edge. It promises to add a powerful boost to the knowledge and anecdotal evidence currently available to grant professionals and nonprofit leaders regarding successful grant seeking.

A third benefit of this book is the funder viewpoint: analyses of several private and community foundations across the nation and Funder Perspectives or interviews related to each factor under review. For the purposes of our research, we have focused heavily on three types of foundations: private foundations, family foundations, and to a lesser degree corporate foundations. A few community foundations have also been profiled, but only those that award discretionary grants independent of their donor-advised funds. The responses of individual foundations can be used to understand how foundations in general make their decisions, and what motivates them to give. Funders may also find these interviews interesting as they seek to improve their own grant making strategies. Foundation officials can use this book as a resource for understanding how nonprofits are continually reinventing themselves and making improvements for the benefit of the people they serve.

## Book Layout

If you are looking for a book on basic grant writing, this is not the one for you. But if you are seeking to take your organization to the next level through sustainable grant seeking practices, you will find the following pages extremely useful. This book is designed to assist nonprofit organizations in the creation of strategies for improving institutional contributions that go beyond the grant writer or even the grants department. It attempts to change the mindset that grant seeking is a staff function and that the responsibility of acquiring grant funds is the sole responsibility of grant professionals (see Figure B).

For this reason, although Chapter 7 offers a refresher course for the writing process, the main thrust of the book is best practices rather than checklists

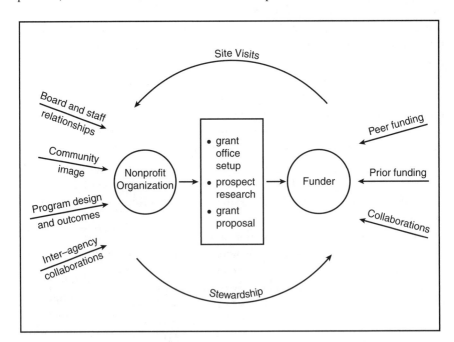

Figure B  *Grant Seeking Strategies*

and lesson plans. One caveat is that a few basic concepts have been elaborated, which many readers may already be familiar with. These concepts have been included only if the topic is of strategic value and correlates with either the research or the underlying theme of the book. Some fundamentals have been included if they belong to a discipline that grant professionals may not be familiar with, such as public relations or evaluation design. Further, some ideas—such as board involvement in relationship building—may be understood by many organizations but not put in practice. In that case, too, these basics have been expounded so that grant professionals can bring evidence-based knowledge back to their leadership. Other than that, this book assumes that you or someone else at your organization already has basic technical grant writing skills.

The book has been laid out into parts, each corresponding to a time period which may be weeks, months, or in some cases even years, and may vary by organization as well as by department within the same organization. Part I is the period before applying for a grant, aptly named "Laying the Groundwork" because it includes chapters related to relationship building, public relations, and program design. These practices should occur well before foundations are approached, and they should be ongoing in nature, meaning that nonprofits should not stop when a proposal has been funded. This part is the longest and has the most chapters—appropriately so, because laying the groundwork is the most important part of any grant seeking strategy and also the least understood and practiced.

Part II deals with "Creating the Request" which should only happen once the homework has been done and all internal and external stakeholders are ready for action. The chapters in this section of the book discuss not only what constitutes a winning grant proposal but also a winning grant writer, whoever it may be in the organization. Since this is not a how-to guide, we have not included every section of a grant proposal in this discussion—only the areas that are most important or which typically are the weakest in terms of writing. With just one chapter about site visits, Part III is thankfully short, since it encompasses the time period called "While the Jury's Out." Finally, Part IV discusses what should occur "After the Grant Award," such as stewardship and reporting, as well as ways of continuing to attract grant investments in the future.

I hope some or all of what lies in these pages will be of use to your organization or your clients. The research findings, best practices, and interviews in this book can help nonprofit leaders and consultants determine agency-wide activities—both short and long term—that support and enhance the efforts of the grant professional. Our data has been collected from a wide variety of organizations ranging from grassroots organizations, community based nonprofits, and faith-based groups to academic institutions and hospitals. While grant professionals working for all sizes and types of nonprofits will most definitely benefit from the findings, the true value of this book lies in the collaboration of almost all departments or functional areas within each nonprofit, including public relations, marketing, programs, and even finance and operations.

## ENDNOTES

Faruqi, S. (2004). Grantee-grantor relationships: a research study. *Journal of the American Association of Grant Professionals*:3(2):37–46.

# Part I

# Laying the Groundwork

# Foster Internal Relationships

> *"Before you contact any foundation, make sure that your own house is in order. One thing that is important to us is that a Board of Directors is giving to its own organization. The nonprofit board today needs to be a fundraising board. If your board is not giving 100%, then why should we?"*
>
> Irene Phelps, President
> Siragusa Foundation

Just like everything else, strategic grant seeking begins with a mindset. Organizations that consider foundation grants to be a staff function are limited to what the staff can achieve alone, whereas those that draw upon the expertise and connections of organizational leaders soar to new heights in grant seeking success. The moment the organizational mindset is expanded to consider funders as partners with the same goals, the significance of involving top leadership becomes apparent. When building collaborations in the field, nonprofits rely on leadership participation—in fact, as we will discuss in later chapters, partnerships within the community are so important that they are often included in strategic planning and outcome measurement. Once partnerships with funders are viewed in a similar light, the contribution of the board and senior staff begins to be truly appreciated and implemented.

## Energizing Leaders

The connections and friendships of a board of directors at personal and professional levels can be extremely helpful in obtaining all types of funding, yet countless organizations have non-fundraising boards. Much has been written about board members' responsibilities as fundraisers, and many books on how to prepare boards to ask for money are available today (1). However, many board members are never urged to fundraise by the staff of charities they are associated with. Consequently, board members of nonprofits often fail to fully understand their main purpose: to go out into the community and raise money or step down. Strong words? Not if you consider the board's responsibility as being equivalent to that of any staff member in the organization: in no circumstances would an agency tolerate a grant writer who did not write well, an accountant who mismanaged funds, or a case manager who abused children. But board members who put in an appearance solely at monthly meetings, or who make excuses when asked to assist in fundraising, are tolerated by their peers as well as by the organizational staff who is well-aware of the negative impact of such lack of engagement.

If a board member does not fully understand or accept this crucial role, putting it in writing as a job description or contract can be helpful. Organizations that expect board members to set goals for themselves and then continually evaluate individual members in areas such as meeting attendance, community activities, and giving find that the motivation and productivity of the board as a whole tends to increase. At The Gathering Place in Houston, TX, the responsibility of the board to fundraise is spelled out in the by-laws, providing board members with absolute clarity about expectations. As a result, approximately 40% of the organization's budget is raised through foundation grants. Going even further, Pitzer College in Claremont, CA, has implemented a "Trustee Report Card" to hold board members accountable to stated responsibilities including meeting attendance and total giving. The report cards are periodically reviewed by the Composition and Procedures Committee as part of the board re-election process; trustees who do not score well can be engaged in discussions and positive encouragement. As a result, the college has found that trustee involvement and motivation levels have increased tremendously (see Figure 1.1).

Nonprofit staff must realize that people typically serve on boards in the hopes of achieving some kind of gain; this may be personal (feeling important, gaining recognition amongst their peers), professional (fulfilling a job requirement, improving professional skills and expertise), or altruistic (contributing to a good cause, religious values). Therefore, in most cases board members want to work and be identified with each other—their peers. Instead of trying to involve each board member in isolation, a better method of encouraging fundraising and grant seeking may be bringing into play positive group dynamics that include other board members, such as committee involvement, peer ratings, and peer encouragement to name a few.

When it comes to grant seeking, nonprofits boards are typically even less involved than in other fundraising roles. A large majority of nonprofit leaders—including staff—think of foundation funders as individuals and institutions that support their programs based on the merits of a grant application.

| Trustee Name | |
|---|---|
| Date | |
| Meetings | Number/percent of board meetings attended: |
| Gifts | Total cash contributions: |
| Pending | Pending pledge amounts: |
| Rating (1–5) | **Category: Governance** |
| | Attended all required meetings |
| | Reviewed any materials provided in advance materials of meetings |
| | Provided input to help the board make good decisions |
| | Served on at least one board committee |
| | Followed all by-laws and board policies |
| | **Category: Contributions** |
| | Contributed financially to the organization with personal resources |
| | Suggested other potential donors and board members |
| | Participated in all fundraising initiatives of the organization |
| | Facilitated connections with own affiliations and the organization |
| | **Category: Volunteerism** |
| | High level of communication and participation within the board |
| | Contributed expertise and knowledge to the organization and the board |
| | Represented the organization in at least one nonboard event in the community |

Figure 1.1 *Sample Trustee Evaluation*

As a result, all contact with current and potential funders before, after, and during the grant seeking process is constrained by this accepted wisdom. Contrary to this type of thinking, foundations are now beginning to ask critical questions regarding applicant nonprofits' board volunteer involvement and financial support and are unwilling to invest in organizations unable to show sufficient contributions by its own leadership. Further, as Chapter 6 explains, a large number of foundations rely heavily on the affiliations and priorities of individual trustees to award grants to nonprofits, and corporate contributions are based in a number of cases on employee recommendations. Hence, the role of the board in enhancing the grant seeking process becomes as important as its role in other areas of fundraising, although the methods employed may be different.

However, the reality is that many volunteer leaders would rather be associated with a special event or a building campaign, because it allows them to sell a "product" such as gala tickets or a named brick in the pavement. Sometimes directors are willing to invite their friends or business associates to the annual

---

## Best Practice: ECHO

ECHO is a nonprofit Christian organization in North Fort Myers, FL, that networks with community leaders in developing countries to seek hunger solutions. Staff leaders aggressively pursue a board education and involvement policy; one method used to involve board members in raising financial resources is the creation of a Focus Committee on Development comprised of board members who are seasoned fundraisers, as well as those who are comparative novices. Committee members are provided with lists of donors to contact several times each month through personal phone calls. Their task is not only to personally thank the donors but also to gather more information about them, such as what motivated them to give, what opinions they have about ECHO, and whether they would like a tour or more information. The responses received and the opportunity to view the organization through the eyes of its donors has proved to be a wonderful experience for board members. Through a peer encouragement system, this committee has shown marvelous results in not only accomplishment of their tasks but in increasing board involvement and excitement about ECHO's work. In most cases, donors who were thanked and given an opportunity to express their opinions increased their giving substantially.

---

gala, but hesitate to approach the trustee of a family foundation to consider a grant proposal. Grant professionals at these organizations often express their frustration at the absence of board assistance and, in some cases, even present resistance to requests for input while submitting grant requests. Our study discovered that only 34% of respondent board members and senior staff were involved in grant solicitation activities such as utilizing personal contacts, writing letters of support, or making face-to-face presentations (see Figure 1.2).

Rather than play the blame game, grant professionals and senior staff should investigate the real reasons behind this lack of participation; every organization has a different set of circumstances, and board members cannot be energized until the whole picture is examined and solutions created. For example, a startup nonprofit may find that its board consists of overworked and uncaring individuals who were pressured into becoming board members without an explanation of responsibilities. Another organization may discover that one or more of its board members are dissatisfied with the way programs are being run but have never received the opportunity to express their feelings. A third organization's board may consist solely of professional experts—such as social workers or engineers—who contribute significantly to program policy but have absolutely no connections with foundations or corporations.

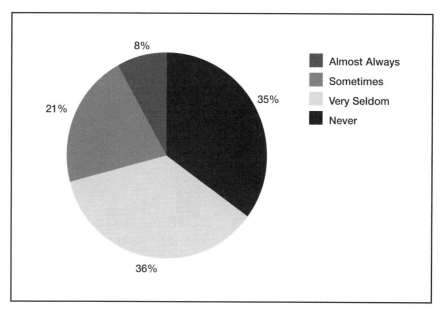

Figure 1.2 *Board & Senior Staff Involved in Grant Solicitation*

In many cases, however, lack of board involvement results from a simple unawareness of the importance of relationships in grant seeking; therefore, the first step in any type of board training or encouragement technique should be an explanation of why and how each board member can leverage his or her connections. For this reason, our research has immense value; grant professionals can use a number of methods—presentations, face-to-face conversations, or strategic planning sessions—to help the board comprehend its role in grant seeking. For instance, our research found that in the case of almost 55% of respondents, a quarter of grants in the last fiscal year were funded as a result of board relationships. Additionally, for more than 15% of respondents, half of all grants received could be attributed to board cultivation (see Figure 1.3).

Further, almost 36% of the organizations surveyed said they have never had a grant declined from a foundation where a board relationship existed. Chances are that the above data will have a powerfully energizing effect on board members as they realize the impact their personal friendships, business connections, and even neighborhood acquaintances can possibly have. It is also important to emphasize to the board, however, that relationship building is hard work and the presence of an affiliation alone is not sufficient to receive a grant. Our research also found that for just over half the respondents, 25% of grants were declined despite the presence of some kind of relationship. Therefore, board members working in conjunction with senior staff and grant professionals must

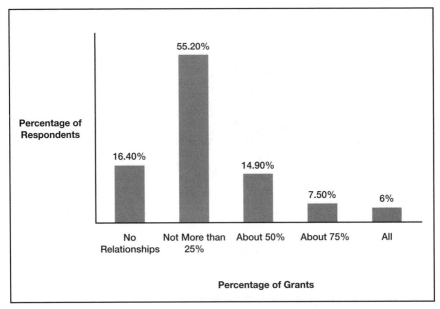

Figure 1.3 *Grants Funded Due to Board Relationships*

explore and cultivate relationships on an ongoing basis in order for the grant function to improve. Chapter 6 includes information about how some organizations are using creative new techniques such as mapping exercises to identify relationships. Although the grant professional in cooperation with fundraising directors must play a key role in this process, other areas of the development department—especially major gifts—can play an important task in training the board in cultivation techniques and how to make the ask.

It is equally important for board members to realize—and for nonprofit staff to help them understand—that relationship building can take many forms. The ideal situation for a nonprofit is to have one or more board members who are foundation trustees or who know such trustees personally. The average grant professional may wonder if that ever actually occurs. In fact, many board members of nonprofits large and small belong to or have personal connections with family foundations or donor-advised funds at community foundations. The people behind these foundations are not billionaires, nor do they necessarily come from historically wealthy families. Many ordinary individuals with a few million in assets have set up family foundations or donor-advised funds in order to have a greater impact and receive tax benefits. Since many do not accept unsolicited proposals, the key to accessing those funds is to connect with these people in a genuine way using current and new board connections. See Chapter 6 for a discussion on the various types of foundations.

Furthermore, organizations in the very early stages of development can sometimes bring in funders, social and community leaders, and corporate officials with relative ease. Having the backing of well-connected individuals who believe in the mission of the organization from the very beginning is the best way to avoid discussions of board responsibilities in the future. Similarly, organizations starting a new project or program can also include funders and community leaders during the planning stages, thereby increasing their chances of continued success. For example, the trustees of smaller family foundations are often personally involved with nonprofits; attempting to build relationships with such people and encouraging their involvement either as board members, advisors, or program volunteers can be very helpful as well. This concept is explained in several chapters later in the book.

One challenge faced by many nonprofit boards is their lack of involvement with programs. In many cases, the extent of a board member's understanding of what occurs in the organization on a daily basis is limited to monthly or quarterly board meetings, updates by the executive director, or information in newsletters. Sometimes senior staff is partly to blame for this arm's length approach, but frequently board members themselves dictate the level of involvement. Consider this: someone who learns about a closing sale at a local furniture store will gladly spread the news to everyone they know, but rarely will they discuss a new retirement plan. The reason: the first is easier to explain and more exciting to share, while the second is complicated and not easily understood. If only the workings of the plan could be explained in plain English and the benefits and rewards clarified, he or she would be thrilled about sharing this good fortune with others. Board members may find themselves in a similar situation and, consequently, be hesitant to involve their friends or colleagues in an organization they themselves are not excited about.

In some cases, board members who *are* engaged may feel exhausted by the continual stream of fundraising activities they already participate in—after all, they have their own professions, families, and other responsibilities to deal with as well. Grant professionals must be understanding of this dilemma faced by many well-meaning board members and try to facilitate the grant seeking process for them as much as possible. If fundraising saturation has occurred, creative ways of remotivation must be considered: for an organization conducting one or more fundraising activities that include board involvement—such as a capital campaign or a special event—it is possible to translate the same excitement into grant seeking by keeping the momentum going after the conclusion of other campaigns. This can be accomplished by offering ongoing board training on fundraising, grant seeking, and on the organization's programs; a necessary component of this continued training is providing grant professionals and other development staff access to their leadership through informal meetings or by encouraging staff to attend certain board meetings.

### Best Practice: JEVS Human Services

JEVS Human Services in Philadelphia, PA, enhances the employability and self-sufficiency of individuals through a broad range of support programs including job readiness, skill development, and vocational rehabilitation. JEVS has a $72 million budget supported primarily through government sources and service fees; individuals and foundations are approached to fund the gaps. As a result, the organization often finds it difficult to motivate board members and make them understand the need for foundation dollars. In order to empower and educate the board, the development staff at JEVS designed short funding profiles for each program that needs funding; the profiles are summaries of larger proposals, clearly and succinctly explaining the programs, target audience, budget, need, and funding gaps. The profiles are collected in loose-leaf binders separated by area of focus; each funding profile is a stand-alone document that can be detached by the board member for his or her use. With the introduction of these funding profiles, the board has become empowered to explain the programs and their needs to potential funders in a way that was not possible before. They find it easier to get a true understanding of the what, why, where, how, and who of the organization's more than 20 different programs and are therefore motivated to assist in fundraising efforts.

Since many Executive Directors remain cautious of unrestricted board–staff interactions, procedures can be put in place to ensure continued success: for example, staff may be requested to inform the Executive Director beforehand of any meetings with board members and to report back with notes or minutes. Additionally, program and development staff may be required to deliver presentations about their areas of responsibility at board meetings. Thirdly, annual meetings may include informal discussions, meet-and-greets, and other avenues for staff to interact with board members without the typical stress of work or deadlines. This type of guided communication allows, among other things, the sharing of knowledge about prospective grantors as well as individual donors who may have foundation connections, and expand the use of moves management (2) from major gifts and annual campaigns to foundation relations.

## Introducing Fresh Faces

If all efforts to identify and utilize connections fail, an organization must realize that the current board setup may not be advantageous from a fundraising perspective. As mentioned earlier, some organizations—typically startups or those located in remote rural areas—have few or no relationships with foundations. In other cases, many nonprofits fail because of a lack of good candidates or a higher priority on programs recruiting board members based on their corporate relationships, or personal connections with community leaders and funders. Our study asked respondents if their boards had good relationships with foundations through personal friendships, family ties, or professional dealings: the results showed that although a large number of did have such connections, most did not (see Figure 1.4).

Contrary to popular opinion, this absence of relationships has nothing to do with the size or age of the organization. Our research found that while many *small budget* organizations had no relationships with foundations at the board level, a higher percentage of *very large budget* organizations also lacked these relationships (24% for small nonprofits versus 41% for very large ones). *Large budget* organizations came in a close second with more than 22% having no board connections (see Figure 1.5).

The effect of the above data is that almost 72% of all organizations without significant relationships received less than a quarter of their funding from foundations. Therefore, it should be recognized that although revitalizing and engaging board members is extremely important, a continual search for connected and eager individuals is just as essential in reviving a jaded board. The Minnesota Council of Nonprofits, like many others, highlights job

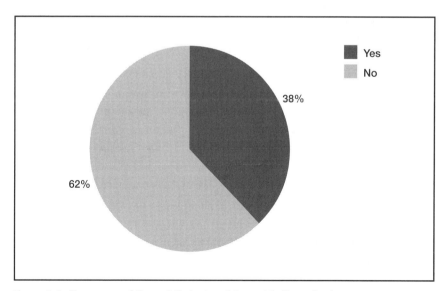

Figure 1.4 *Presence of Board Relationships with Foundations*

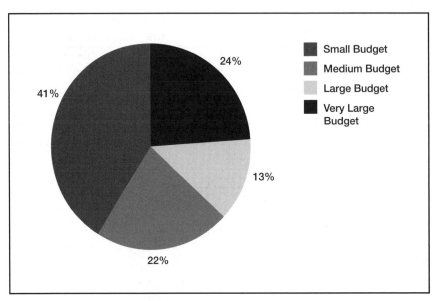

Figure 1.5 *Respondents Having No Board Relationships by Size*

descriptions of key leadership positions as well as personal characteristics to consider when choosing board members (3). Such resources can be helpful to organizations willing to bring in fresh blood and new perspectives. However, many nonprofits argue that finding and retaining good board members is like swimming against the current: it requires intense effort with very little chance of success. Although the quality of the board member can certainly not be guaranteed, numerous avenues exist for identifying high quality candidates:

1.  Board Match programs sponsored by local United Ways and volunteer centers throughout the country; for example, the Center for Nonprofit Effectiveness in Miami offers frequent Meet & Greet receptions to introduce nonprofits to business leaders and community volunteers interested in serving as board members.

2.  An organization's external stakeholders, such as community partners, bankers, and insurance agents who may have emerging leaders on staff.

3.  Local business groups, such as chambers of commerce or networking associations of young lawyers or medical professionals.

4.  Previous clients or others who have been positively impacted by the organization.

5.  Foundation staff with whom relations are already strong enough to take to the next level of involvement.

Deciding who to invite to serve on the board is an important strategic decision for an organization; how it operates, how the outside community views it, and what its future holds depends greatly on the quality of the board members it attracts. If grant professionals are involved in this strategic decision-making process, they may be able to help find volunteers of the highest caliber based on their knowledge of funders—both foundation and corporate. For example, an adult literacy organization may benefit a great deal from inviting an employee of Dollar General to sit on its board because of the high priority placed by that company on that particular cause and the large amount of financial support it gives each year to similar organizations. Many times, the skills or expertise of an individual board member—say an accounting executive or a small business owner—may not have the same impact in terms of future grant awards as an employee of a larger company who at first glance does not seem to "fit." In many nonprofits, only the grant professional has access to such information—another reason why open communications between departments as well as with leaders is important for organizational well-being.

Recognizing that volunteers, other than board members, can also be a source of wealth and connections, organizations should bring in new people through a variety of volunteer opportunities. Some volunteers may show potential but their lack of experience may preclude them from joining a board of directors; such professionals can be invited to join an advisory committee or a young leaders circle instead. Although it takes time and effort to polish these individuals and teach them the ins and outs of the organization, they can ultimately form a well-qualified pool of board candidates. While they gain experience they can utilize their employment or social groups to raise money by organizing special events or annual gifts.

A classic example of this type of leadership development program is Big Brothers Big Sisters of Metro Atlanta, GA, which utilizes a guild of young professionals called the "BBBS Ambassadors" to hold fundraisers and build community relationships. The annual fundraiser held by this group is aptly titled "The Big Event." Many similar groups exist across the country with the aim of advancing the parent agency's agenda—both program-wise and through fundraising—and offering networking opportunities among themselves. The Buffalo Bayou Partnership in Houston, TX, has the "Bayou Buddies," a membership-based affiliate with its own steering committee and quarterly newsletters. It brings "like-minded green enthusiasts" together for volunteer events as well as social gatherings.

Although guilds and young professional societies are old friends of the fundraising department, grant professionals often do not consider them important to grant seeking success. Consider the model suggested by this book: that grant seeking is a critical element of the overall development plan and must work in conjunction with other development areas as well as other organizational departments in order to be successful. Ideas and techniques traditionally used by other fundraising areas can easily be adapted by grant professionals or at least be used as a way to improve revenue from grants in the long run. Therefore, guild or advisory members who attend happy hours or clean up beaches may be up-and-coming professionals with potential in their companies, and may have connections with foundations at the family and corporate level. Granted, these connections may not currently be strong enough to bring in large dollar amounts, but the groundwork laid now will reap rewards in the future when a committee member advances to the trustee level in his or her family foundation or a promotion results in a position on the charitable contributions committee. It is important to be very selective and strategic in choosing members of advisory committees and guilds, and it is certainly permissible to inform prospective members about expectations of current and future support.

Advisory boards may also be created for the opposite reason: involving respected community leaders who have resources and connections but not the desire to serve on a board and take on added responsibility. Teen Lifeline in Phoenix, AZ, has created an Advisory Council consisting of a few high-profile individuals—such as the mayor, local television personalities, and high profile business men—who are willing to open their checkbooks or make phone calls on behalf of the organization. One new member is selected each year through presentation of the Community Lifeline Award, and award recipients commit to serving on the Advisory Council. For Teen Lifeline, which has an operating budget of less than $500,000, the support provided by this high-powered group of individuals is critical.

Grant professionals must also remember that foundation trustees and community leaders are not the only source of grant funds; in fact, corporate volunteers are often an underutilized resource in grant seeking. A recent study of 36 Excellent Employee Volunteer Programs (EVPs) by the Points of Light Foundation discovered that 56% of Excellent EVPs provide release time to their employees for volunteering, and 58% offer grants to the organizations where employees volunteer. Further, 67% have formal award programs honoring employee volunteering that involve grants to nonprofits selected by the honorees. Not surprisingly, almost every corporate foundation or charitable giving arm of a company prefers to give to nonprofits where their employees are involved, yet nonprofits sometimes are not aware of the companies represented by their volunteer base or the grant opportunities available through these individuals. Organizations that understand the significance of corporate volunteerism often possess too narrow a perspective and focus their energies solely on board member affiliations. However, some non-board volunteers are often more committed to the organizations they serve because they perform their duties without the prestige of a label. This commitment can be leveraged into dollars if the time and effort is taken to get to know them and their employers. Many nonprofits have corporate involvement events—such as "Bowl for Kids' Sake" events by many Big Brothers Big Sisters affiliates spanning weeks or even months—but few take advantage of the excitement generated by these events to attract and retain high-quality volunteers for ongoing grant seeking activities.

The above issue compels communication between programs and grant writing staff, because of the need to track volunteer hours and corporate affiliations. Systems, whether based on technology or paper, must be put into place so that the grants team is alerted of new volunteers as well as changes in current volunteer employers and positions.

For the sake of simplicity, take the example of Mr. Smith and Ms. Doe, both of whom have mentored clients in a job training program every weekend for the last six months. Mr. Smith previously worked at ABC Corporation, which does not match volunteer hours nor give grants to nonprofits. But, last month he got a job at XYZ Inc. as an associate. XYZ Inc. is well-known in the nonprofit community for its matching grants program, in-kind donation program, and cash grants program. Ms. Doe has already been working at XYZ Inc. as a Department Head for the last 15 years.

Needless to say, both Mr. Smith and Ms. Doe can be assets to the organization where they volunteer because of their professional affiliations—but only if the grant professional is aware of several things:

1. Mr. Smith's job change from ABC Corporation to XYZ Inc.
2. Mr. Smith's new position and the fact that as a new employee in a junior level he cannot seek grant funds, but can support a request for donated computers.
3. Ms. Doe's senior level position, which could result in an invitation to sit on the nonprofit's board or advisory committee, chair its gala, or write a letter of support for a major grant application.
4. XYZ Inc.'s policies for charitable contributions and volunteerism.

It seems simple enough, yet how many times do grant writers—or even program staff—track when a volunteer changes his or her job? Unless the volunteer happens to be a board member, chances are that this valuable information will never reach the organization. All organizations should have some means of recording employer information for their volunteers and updating it on a regular basis. This could be through quarterly surveys tied to volunteer recognition, reminders in monthly e-newsletters, or through one additional question asked by a case worker checking up on her case load. Further, volunteer orientation or regular training could be used to ensure that volunteers agency-wide understand the importance of tracking volunteer hours, reporting to their employers and informing the nonprofits they serve of any internal decisions that could help potential grant applications. Lastly, only if cooperation and communication exists between the development and program staff will such information when presented be compiled and forwarded to the grants team; it is essential, therefore, that discussion about the implementation and tracking of such data should form a regular part of organizational practices.

## Motivating Staff

A third source of relationships often not understood or considered relevant is nonprofit staff. Some organizations are fortunate enough to have senior management such as an Executive Director or CEO with connections in the funding community; these may be a result of prior affiliations or through active efforts at socializing and networking as part of their job description. Unfortunately, countless Executive Directors focus exclusively on programs and day-to-day operations—due to either a lack of resources to hire additional staff, or because of Founder's Syndrome (5)—and may be leaving many relationship building opportunities on the table. The absence of staff connections, our research found, is quite prevalent (see Figure 1.6):

- 33% of *small budget* organizations possessed no senior staff relationships.
- 42% of *very large budget* organizations had no such relationships.
- 72% of respondents without staff connections with funders said they received less than a quarter of their income from foundations.

Another interesting fact uncovered by the research was this: nonprofits that had board connections had almost double the senior staff relations with funders (81%) as compared to nonprofits without board connections (42%). This finding may hold the key to the impact of senior staff relationships on the entire organization: board relationships may be more important in terms of money raised, but senior staff must pave the way and set an example by becoming involved in this process first. Only then will they have the desire and means to transform their leadership. Very rarely do nonprofits emerge into existence with high-powered boards, yet executive directors or CEOs can begin fostering relationships within their communities and with potential funders almost from day one. In some instances, however, the reverse also holds true: active board members can either persuade staff to become involved or to leave the organization, paving the way for more motivated personnel to enter. This should be food for thought for organizations that make excuses about the use of senior staff time only for program or administrative duties.

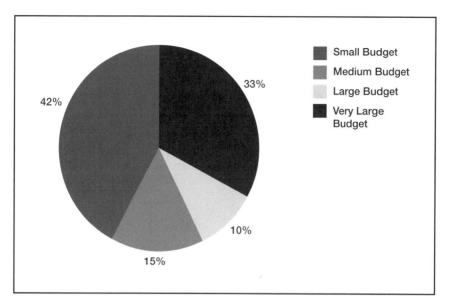

Figure 1.6 *Respondents Having No Senior Staff Relationships by Size*

Typically, the larger the organization, the more time the executive director or CEO spends on relationship-building, because more resources are available to hire lower level staff for programmatic or administrative duties. However, in these larger institutions, oftentimes other senior staff members such as program vice presidents or directors fail to take a similar approach, leaving relationship building and public relations efforts to the agency head and relevant departmental staff. This attitude is dangerous for many reasons: program heads may become micro-managers, or a serious disconnect may arise between an organization's public face and its internal functioning. As Chapter 2 will explain, building and improving an organization's community image is the responsibility of all staff, volunteers, and even clients. In the smallest of nonprofits, this approach is often adopted out of necessity, as every hand is expected to be on deck and pulling its own weight in bringing in new board members, donors, and volunteers.

The following chapters of this book will elaborate on some key issues touched upon here and how to move forward with the creation and establishment of grant seeking strategies for your organization. Bear in mind, however, that the elements discussed in this chapter—utilizing existing relationships with funders through three key types of people within your organization—should be addressed first before the factors in subsequent chapters can have the biggest impact.

## ENDNOTES

(1) See List of Suggested Resources.

(2) A strategic and targeted set of actions and contacts designed to bring donors closer to a gift.

(3) Minnesota Council of Nonprofits, Governance: Templates and Samples. www.mncn. org/info/template_gov.htm

(4) Policies and Procedures of the Best Employee Volunteer Programs. Benchmarks of Excellence Series, Points of Light Foundation. www.pointsoflight.org

(5) Founder's Syndrome is a pattern of negative or undesirable behavior by the founder(s) of an organization, after its initial growth when its mission evolves beyond what they originally had in mind.

# Chapter 1 Checklist

## Organizational Readiness

| Indicator | Status |
|---|---|
| Are board members aware of our grant seeking activities? | |
| Do board members understand our programs and services? | |
| Is there an evaluation system such as job descriptions, contracts, or report cards for the board? | |
| Do board members give personal or professional referrals to foundations and corporations for grant seeking? | |
| Are new members invited to serve on the board on a regular basis? | |
| Do grant professionals and other staff members have contact with board members? | |
| Do we have a guild or advisory board to recruit and train potential board members? | |
| Are employees of our area's large companies involved as volunteers of our organization? | |
| Does senior staff build and cultivate relationships with foundations on a regular basis? | |
| Do individual staff members have opportunities and time for networking and relationship building? | |

## Grant Professional Readiness

| Indicator | Status |
|---|---|
| Am I aware of individual board members' personal and professional contacts with foundations and corporations? | |
| Do I have regular contact with the board's executive and/or fundraising committee? | |
| Am I involved in board education or training as it relates to the grant seeking process? | |
| Do I work with other development staff to create cultivation strategies that include foundations? | |
| Do I research community leaders and corporate volunteers who may serve on our board or guild and inform my leadership about these potential contacts? | |
| Do I work with program staff to monitor corporate volunteer involvement and changes? | |

# Develop Community Image

> "At many foundations, program officers as well as trustees have
> on-the-ground relationships with nonprofits. They often make fund-
> ing decisions by hearing of nonprofits through word of mouth, and
> by networking with other foundations to share their knowledge of the
> nonprofit sector. If I as a program officer am funding an organization, it is
> because I believe in what it is doing; therefore I will tell others about it and
> spread the word on its behalf. That's the best PR a nonprofit can get."
>
> Kerrie Blevins, Foundation Director
> The Patrick and Aimee Butler Family Foundation

No matter how unfair it may seem, public perception is often a big factor playing into the success or failure of an organization. The media holds a powerful role in educating the public—whether correctly or incorrectly—about the internal workings of both corporate and nonprofit entities. In recent times, oversight and governance have become big issues for nonprofits to conquer; the communities and governments they serve have begun to ask serious questions about accountability and social responsibility. Although the general opinion in the nonprofit community is that marketing is a business tool and that money spent on it could be better utilized for programs, wise nonprofit leaders understand that public relations are fundamental to fundraising and friend-raising. Such leaders therefore aim to make strategic decisions about their public relations efforts and involve not just the marketing staff but also programs and development.

# Got Mission?

Mission statements are a big part of any nonprofit organization, and grant professionals in particular use them almost every day as they craft proposals and other written pieces that reach out to the public. Workshops and courses on every aspect of nonprofit management deal with crafting the mission statement in a way that explains succinctly the true reason why the organization exists. But in many cases, mission statements become mere statements over the years, no longer real indicators of the values and purpose of the organization. In other situations, missions are so ambiguous and full of legalese that they boggle the mind of the reader and explain nothing. If the staff or volunteers of an organization are asked what their mission is, they use words and explanations very different from the actual statement.

Before embarking upon a public relations effort that attempts to attract the community, it is important to not only be aware internally of what an organization's mission is, but to embody it externally as well. When a nonprofit is born, its founders and other involved persons have a certain idea of its purpose and intentions, but as time passes, that purpose may change based on the realities of working in the field or due to a better understanding of the issues faced by the community being served. In many cases, a reassessment of the mission and vision of each organization becomes necessary after some years and may need to occur fairly regularly. This re-evaluation could easily be implemented in strategic planning sessions if an organization conducts those on a consistent basis—after all, it is the fundamental from which other strategies such as program goals, action plans, and even fundraising plans should be derived. If strategic planning is not an option, then some other type of methodology must be adopted—perhaps in the form of interviews, surveys, or smaller departmental meetings that pose a series of questions and brainstorm ideas. The mission's revision may also become necessary for an organization that undergoes major changes in structure or leadership—such as the founder retiring from the helm after 20 years or an entirely new service being offered for the first time—or only because a need is felt for renewed drive and enthusiasm among staff and volunteers. Certainly our recommendations in Chapter 1 for engaging current board members and introducing fresh faces will serve an organization well as it re-examines its mission.

For several reasons, grant professionals should remain at the forefront of this reassessment: oftentimes they are the only ones within the organization using the mission statement on a consistent basis. In their conversations with funders, they are typically asked questions related to their organization's purpose and vision for the future, and they are aware of the organization's programs and administration from a holistic viewpoint rather than from the narrower perspective that department heads may possess. Grant professionals can also benefit from discussions about mission and can improve their writing and funder interactions by understanding the relationship between mission and programs. As an example, potential funders of faith-based organizations—discussed in more detail in Chapter 7—often have questions about faith and secularism that may be difficult to answer in grant applications or during site visits. The YMCA of Greater Cincinnati explains this very well on their website by asking "where is the C in YMCA?" For grant professionals as well as others who may not find it easy to connect a Christian mission to the physical and emotional programming offered by the Y, it explains the connection from a programming aspect; for example: "confessing that we are our brother's keepers as we contribute to programs for under privileged youth." By similarly explaining the programs in relation to the overall mission or vision, an organization can educate not only funders but also insiders who may not know or have simply forgotten.

Why is mission evaluation so significant to the development of community image? While many explanations exist, the most important one is that an organization that no longer externally reflects its purpose and goals is in danger of being viewed negatively by the community it operates in. External reflection therefore does not only mean emblazoning the mission statement in grant proposals and letterhead or quoting it in speeches made by the executive director. Each and every contact with the community at large by any person associated by the organization should automatically reflect its mission. Bike Pittsburgh, for instance, has board members who show their passion everyday by hiking, cycling to work, racing mountain bikes, and even proudly riding the bus. They are avid advocates of the nonprofit not because they are on the board but because it comes naturally to them. Remaining true to an organization's mission may be as simple as a senior citizens center offering bigger font or audio capabilities on its website or a children's nonprofit providing day care for its employees on site. If the culture of the organization is such that its values and spirit are understood and agreed upon by all, the public will have no choice but to sit up and take notice because the everyday actions of its staff and volunteers will be a physical embodiment of its mission and values.

One method of implementing the above concept is to include organizational values and goals in employee and volunteer performance measurement, and grant professionals are in an excellent position to advocate this approach. Knowing that funders will appreciate the inclusion of such measurement, they can assist in the creation of specific goals and objectives that will help demonstrate a commitment to providing services of the highest quality. These goals could relate to safety, customer appreciation, prompt response, or any other indicator that is a part of the service being provided by the nonprofit. Service delivery models can be expanded to include these aspects: for example, case workers taking 24 hours or less to respond to inquiries, volunteers receiving an A+ in satisfaction surveys by clients, or organizations receiving consistent ratings in national, state, or local recognitions. It goes without saying that positive results of any such performance measurements should be broadcast not only in public relations activities but also in grant proposals to foundations.

When crafting a mission statement in itself or as part of more comprehensive strategic planning, it is essential to seek the input of all stakeholders; volunteers and clients, for example, can contribute valuable insight of how the organization is viewed by the public or what areas need improvement. Methods of doing so abound, from the inexpensive to the very costly. Typically, walk-in comment cards, online surveys, or focus groups are all cost-effective ways to collect a host of information with which to move forward. The Interfaith Council for Peace and Justice in Ann Arbor, MI, consulted its constituents through a listening project consisting of 130 surveys and 6 listening sessions in order to ask questions such as "what do you care about most?," "what do you see as the most important elements of our work?," and "how do you see us balancing multiple issues with the need to focus?" The result was a 51-page document full of data that prompted a shift in focus and policies related to their Middle East work and improvements in program design. Leaders of the organization report an increase in funding after the listening project and attribute it to mission clarity. Similarly, at Pitzer College in Claremont, CA, participation and social responsibility are core values. Rather than mere lip service or small social efforts on an individual level, the college has included broad community input from students, faculty, staff, and alumni for major building projects. Further, the community's voice has been incorporated in many aspects of decision-making, including the green planning process for sustainable building.

Within the organization, all such strategy sessions should involve grant professionals as well as other department workers for open discussions. Grant professionals can bring the opinions of funders to the table and can address any conflicting issues raised while writing grant proposals; for example, they are often in an ideal position to ask whether certain programs align themselves with the overall mission and purpose of the organization. Knowing how important board involvement is from a funder's perspective, grant professionals can lead the way in encouraging board members to identify with the mission and brainstorm ways to excite passion for their cause. When discussing improvements in programs or management, grant professionals armed with the appropriate prospect research tools can offer valuable advice on how to improve quality of service or create targeted public relations efforts that will positively affect institutional grants and donations. Working together with grant professionals, program staff can assess collaboration opportunities, create appropriate program goals and objectives, and discuss the expanded role of volunteers in programs.

# Blow Your Own Horn

Once every staff member and volunteer within an organization is excited about what the organization does and plans to do in the future, the next step is to create a comprehensive public relations plan or to re-evaluate an existing one. Many books and online resources are available to help guide this process; however, some aspects of a public relations plan are conducive to interdepartmental input including that of grant professionals. Stephens College in Columbia, MO, celebrated its 175th anniversary in 2008 not just through marketing, but by conducting outreach on a national level with the hope of increasing awareness and community pride. As part of this celebration, they profiled several alumni as "amazing women" in local magazines and through their website. These alumni include actresses, scientists, and corporate and nonprofit leaders. They also produced an event called the "High Heeled Leader" where the college president opened up to audiences about her experiences, leadership style, and accomplishments.

## Best Practice: Brighter Beginnings

As part of a strategic planning process, the Oakland, CA, nonprofit The Perinatal Council determined that they needed to build greater community awareness by adopting branding that more clearly reflected their broad range of services and evolving mission. Utilizing volunteer marketing experts, the management decided to conduct a marketing audit to better understand public perception of their services. Thirty people connected with the organization—clients, funders, and former board members—participated in interviews answering questions related to their understanding of services provided and effect in the community. As a result of the audit, the organization changed its name to Brighter Beginnings, created a more attractive logo, and a new visual identity including the look and content of newsletters, its website, and other published materials. A new vision statement was adopted and became part of the new tagline "every family matters." The name change was communicated to foundation funders through a letter explaining the strategic plan and the subsequent improvements. Brighter Beginnings has found that this transformation in image has resulted in greater donor loyalty and increased donations since 2007, as well as a nomination for the 2008 Excellence in Marketing Award (nonprofit category) from the San Francisco chapter of the American Marketing Association.

There are countless creative ways to build a positive community image using both traditional and innovative public relations activities. The key to their success is to provide easy access to information about the organization for the press, both current and potential donors, volunteers, and any other stakeholders who may need it. This means cleaning up the website, creating an online or print press kit, providing in-depth information about programs, and much more. It also includes creating consistent branding and messaging by using the same colors, logos, taglines, and content on both print stationery and online.

Some nonprofits receive substantial publicity for a variety of reasons. Our research found that 49.7% of survey respondents received five or more incidences of initiated publicity in the last fiscal year, such as public service announcements and press releases being picked up by the media. Only 5.8% of respondents received no initiated publicity at all. Of the respondent receiving five or more incidences of publicity, 24.4% were *large budget* organizations, while 60.3% were *very large budget* organizations (See Figure 2.1).

While this points to the greater resources that very large nonprofits may have in terms of marketing or public relations activities, it also may imply that they are well-known in the community as a result of mission alignment and a higher level of expertise in providing services. These respondents also conduct more active grant seeking efforts: a larger number have relationships with foundations at the board and senior staff level compared to the total and reach out more to foundation grantors during the year in nonsoliciting activities.

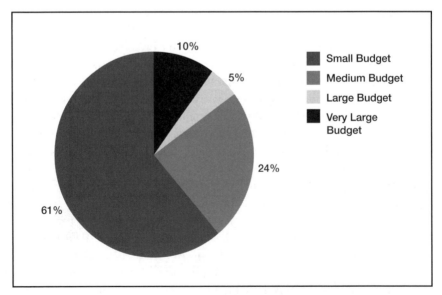

Figure 2.1 *Respondents Receiving More Than 5 Incidences of Publicity by Size*

On the other hand, organizations receiving no publicity took fewer opportunities for overall communication and outreach to donors: 37.5% never contacted a foundation grantor for nonsoliciting purposes during the year, as opposed to 1.3% of those who received the greatest number of publicity incidences, and 8.2% of all respondents of the survey. This further points to fewer grant strategies at all budgetary levels, combined with less overall communication for the entire organization (See Figure 2.2).

Reaching out to foundation donors for public relations purposes is a very delicate road: nonprofits often inundate their funders with newsletters, invitations to events, and the like in the hopes of generating interest that may translate into funding. Unfortunately, program officers and trustees rarely have the time or motivation to read publications or give personal appearances unless there is a deeper relationship between the grantor and grantee. Later in this chapter, as well as in Chapters 9 and 10, we discuss how to engage and involve foundations and other stakeholders through targeted communications and outreach plans that involve programs and development. Grant professionals who are allowed access to activities traditionally earmarked for marketing can help improve the entire public relations effort by alerting them to key issues raised by funders. One of my clients was asked recently by a foundation reviewing their proposal why the number of low-income clients served had

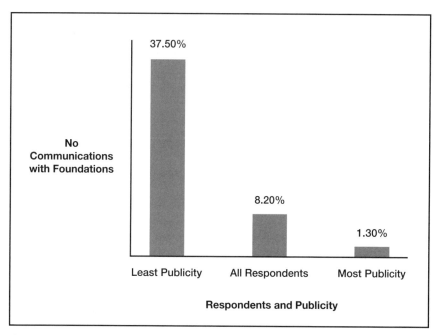

Figure 2.2 *Percentage of Respondents Never Communicating with Foundations*

decreased from the year before. A donor may very well have the same question when program numbers are highlighted in an annual report or online, but unless the grant professional is consulted, the marketing staff may not even realize the significance of this question. Other issues include the ratio of funds spent on programs as opposed to fundraising and administration, program accomplishments related to goals and outcomes, and expertise of key staff and volunteers—all are items that may be missed by marketing staff attempting to create newsletters, fact sheets, annual reports, or websites in a vacuum. While database software may give names and amounts for the donor roll, the human

## Funder Perspective: The St. Paul Foundation
*Trista Harris, Former Program Officer*

Q: How effective do you think nonprofit public relations efforts are?
A: For a lot of organizations, public relations focuses on volume—for example, tons of newsletters. If you're sending slick newsletters, some foundations may feel you have enough money and don't need their funding. To me, it's more about the work you're doing. What is really helpful is when an organization is conducting systems change, they create research reports, for example, how to use incarceration rates, and look outside their own work. For example, an organization working in early education looked at the whole process and wanted to get the data out to the community. Public relations should be about a nonprofit's place in the world, not just about them individually. Good research reports and articles are helpful to us because we learn about trends through them and are able to connect to a number of nonprofits that we would otherwise not know about.

For foundation staff, events are less helpful. I get approximately 15 invitations each week and part of it is that I don't feel it's fair to go to one organization's event and not the other's. For a nonprofit whose proposal is pending or for a recent grantee, I may attend an event in order to find out more information outside of the proposal. For example, I recently attended a grand opening celebration of a building which we funded, because I wanted to see how it turned out. Also, I may visit a nonprofit to see how it functions when the public is present; for example, we recently funded a new community center and I wanted to learn what the community felt about it, hear their comments, and see the building actually being used. That way I can give honest feedback to our board—word on the street is always more valuable than chicken dinners. Such events also allow me to see the interaction between staff and clients, which can be very useful when reviewing proposals.

touch provided by stories of family foundation trustees can only be provided by grant professionals who are capturing that information year-round. On the other hand, grant professionals can improve their own proposals by borrowing the brand and image used for public relations efforts by using taglines on cover pages and including pictures, stories, or letters as appendices.

# Programs and Public Relations

In direct contrast to traditional marketing, organizations fare better in terms of building community image when their public relations efforts center on program activities. This may be as simple as celebrating a milestone: the National Suicide Prevention Lifeline answering the one millionth call to their suicide hotline, or Lutheran Social Services in Austin, TX, placing their 7,000th adoption. Other activities take longer to execute but may have income opportunities as well: the board of directors of Wellspring House in Gloucester, MA, asked one of its founders, Rosemary Luling Haughton, to write a short history of the organization; the result: "The Wellspring Story," which is sold at Wellspring events and at their administrative offices. Similarly, a film crew accompanying Interplast volunteer surgeons to Vietnam documented the team's experiences to produce "A Story of Healing," which earned the 1997 Academy Award for best documentary, short subject. The 28-minute film is now available online for free, although donations are encouraged.

Grant professionals should keep track of program-related snippets of information in a centralized location—either physical or virtual—not just to alert the marketing team as needed, but also in order to include them in grant proposals, funding reports, and other contacts with foundations. This may take some concerted effort on the part of both the grants team as well as the program staff, hence sending out periodic inquiries via email or convening informal meetings to brainstorm ideas for potential funder-appropriate public relations activities may be advisable.

Some events may be related to showcasing program results and there-fore also need the coordination of both grant professionals and program staff—not just for the production of the event but also to ensure that grantors and potential funders are invited. I Have a Dream Houston publicizes the results of their program evaluation annually through an event called "Year in the Dream" attended by an audience of donors, volunteers, and community leaders. Although the event does serve as a cultivation tool to find new donors, its main purpose is to demonstrate to funders the impact of their contributions. Underwritten by a corporate sponsor, the event is free and no solicitation occurs during the proceedings.

With the growth of online public relations tools, many organizations are turning to the Internet to engage new audiences and improve their image in the broader community. Blogs can be helpful for publicizing activities and events, such as the education and community programs blog of the Walker Arts Center in Minneapolis, MN, and for highlighting program events in a way that bring them to life, such as volunteers of Project Hope documenting their experiences during humanitarian trips to other countries. Not every blog, e-newsletter, or networking tool is created equal; however, it is important to remember to remain donor-centric and even in many cases differentiate among them based on the target audience. Again, the grant professional can offer immense help to the marketing department with regards to insight and information about institutional donors and their preferences.

### Best Practice: Bike Pittsburgh

Being a membership organization, Bike Pittsburgh values the participation of their constituents in guiding the direction and goals of the organization. When strategic planning was initiated in 2008, it was decided to create a process that was as transparent as possible and to involve the entire constituency in order to get the benefit of everyone's input. Therefore, a kickoff meeting was announced, and members of the public were invited to attend. For those who could not attend, comments and suggestions were encouraged in advance through email. The meeting was attended by approximately 40 members of the public—members who wanted to have a say in what Bike Pittsburgh was doing or planned to do in the future. In addition, the meeting was attended by the board of directors and selected people from the community such as those working at other nonprofits, community leaders, students, and other bike enthusiasts. As a result of this kickoff meeting and the subsequent strategic planning process, the organization created a comprehensive plan of action for the future, with long, medium, and short term goals. The results were summarized into a one-page document called the Strategic Plan Summary, listing three main goals or areas of concern for Bike Pittsburgh. Not only has the strategic plan helped the organization's internal operations by making staff and volunteers more focused, but it has also formed their public relations effort. It is used as a public relations tool to introduce Bike Pittsburgh to the community and to solicit comments and feedback. It is taken along to meetings and handed out at events as part of our outreach effort and aims to make the entire organization more transparent to the public.

Programs that possess a high degree of community outreach or involvement can also be used indirectly for the purpose of building community image, as long as care is taken to ensure that they remain programmatic in nature. The People's Grocery in West Oakland, CA, holds monthly "Grub Parties," that offer free cooking demonstrations, musical performances and interactive discussions to build community awareness around the issue of healthy eating. In addition to the targeted demographic, people from other communities frequently attend to learn more about the organization; often these attendees become donors or volunteers.

Although publicity is mostly beneficial to nonprofits, there can be times when staff and volunteers may prefer to remain unexposed. Negative publicity resulting from a crisis, both internal and external, can have disastrous effects on the reputation of an organization. A well-thought out crisis management plan is essential to ensure that operations continue in times of adversity and that funding and public opinion remains unaffected as much as possible. A few years ago, Stephens College experienced financial troubles due to lagging enrollment; instead of ignoring the issue, their leaders chose to address the crisis in front of current and potential funders—even those who were unaware of it. In these conversations, the college communicated the progress that had been made due to a new presidency, as well as the improvements in enrollment, staff, and programs. Further, funders who arrived for a site visit were shown buildings that had been closed down during the financial crisis in order to bring home the need for their support.

In the wake of several reports of fraud, mismanagement, and general non-stewardship of public trust, many nonprofits face tough questions and guilt by association from their communities. With the passing of the Sarbanes-Oxley Act for corporate entities, nonprofits also face higher expectations and stricter guidelines even though they are currently exempt from most of the provisions of the act. For instance, independent audits, while not required for smaller nonprofits, are essential to maintain the fiscal integrity of an organization; the creation of an audit committee to oversee this process can do wonders in this regard. The American Institute of Certified Public Accountants has created an Audit Committee Toolkit for Not-for-Profit Organizations, with recommendations on how to form and adhere to stated audit and other policies. Other essential, although not required, policies include those addressing conflicts of interest, disclosure, and whistle blowing. The Board Source and the Independent Sector published a paper titled The Sarbanes-Oxley Act and Implications for Nonprofit Organizations, an excellent description of how nonprofits of all sizes can voluntarily adopt governance best practices.

Negative publicity resulting from a regional or national issue—such as product recalls and health scares—can actually serve as positive influences on the public profile of associated charities in some cases. For example, the 2008 salmonella outbreak in the peanut butter industry paved the way for a high profile crisis management solution by the American Peanut Council, including frequent press releases and updates. Similarly, the American Veterinary Medical Association received the 2007 Nonprofit Public Relations Award for Crisis Management during the 2007 pet food recall.

Creative tactics can make even the most mundane of nonprofit events seem interesting and can lead to excitement on the part of the media and the community. The Pennsylvania Convention Center celebrated its expansion in 2007 with a demolition event witnessed by hundreds. Supporters watched as a 200-foot kite string attached to the key to the expansion door was cut to activate the first smash by a 2000-plus pound wrecking ball into the roof of a three-story brick building.

# Experts in the Field

While initiated publicity through press releases, publications, and the like may establish image, true credibility comes by being viewed as an expert in one's field. Expertise may come from individuals—staff and volunteers—associated with an organization and holding a reputation for knowledge and skills specific to a certain area. For this reason, hospitals spend considerable resources on recruiting a high cadre of physicians, and academic institutions proudly announce the credentials of their professors. The staff and volunteers of smaller nonprofits can also take steps to establish credibility and expertise. The Westside Infant-Family Network in Culver City, CA, hires therapists with Master's level or higher education and at least 10 years of experience and displays their credentials and prior experience visibly on the website and in published materials. On the other hand, many organizations with highly experienced and knowledgeable staff do not realize that displaying these individuals' expertise will lend credibility to an organization. Grant professionals often do not take the time to uncover such information either; however, a section on key personnel or human resource capabilities should always be included in proposals, whether required by a foundation or not. A good way to keep abreast of this type of information is to require all staff and key volunteers to submit a bio-data to the grants department. Once polished, this information can also be sent to the marketing or public relations department to include on the website or in other types of materials. A simple questionnaire as below can be developed by the grants professional and circulated among new employees and volunteers, with updates requested on an annual basis.

**Name:**
**Title:**

*Please provide brief answers to the following questions. Please also attach your most recent resume if available.*

**Education:**
Highest degree earned: _____
Institution: _____
Concentration/Major: _____
Other diplomas, certifications, or courses related to current occupation:

_____
_____
_____

**Experience:**
Title at most recent prior job: _____
Organization: _____
Major duties:

_____
_____
_____

Other relevant positions and/or jobs:

_____
_____

Any awards, commendations, or honors relevant to current position:

_____
_____
_____

Figure 2.3 *Bio-Data Worksheet*

Blogs, as mentioned earlier, can also establish the credibility of nonprofit staff and volunteers, such as ECHO's blog postings by the director of their Department of Agricultural Resources on technical topics and specialized areas of agriculture. Other more traditional methods of establishing expertise are through speaking engagements and award nominations; staff and volunteers should always be on the lookout for conferences pertaining to their field of interest and should apply to participate on high level committees outside of their own organizations. This will lead to a gradual image-building not only on a personal level but more importantly for the benefit of the organization.

Many nonprofits also create advisory boards consisting of experts that are not engaged in day-to-day operations but lend their reputation and advice on issues of importance. For example, community health organizations with lesser-known staff or volunteers may be able to find recognized physicians to act as advisors on a specific project or on ongoing concerns. Grant professionals can play an essential role in the identification of experts in the foundation community with expertise in specific social issues, as detailed in board of director recruitment strategies in Chapter 1. The flip side of client or public advisory boards to improve programs or grantseeking efforts will be discussed in Chapter 5.

Further, expertise can be established on an organizational level in several ways. The first is through advocacy efforts, which are mostly defined within the mission or programs of certain organizations. Although several advocacy nonprofits are highly well-known, organizations with community-based programs can also assist in legal or legislative advocacy efforts despite having a programmatic focus. Nonprofit advocacy is important because it attempts to solve major issues on a local, regional or national level—the same issues that nonprofit staff attempt to solve on an organizational level. Girls Incorporated in New York, NY, and the Edgewood Center for Children and Families in the San Francisco Bay Area, CA, are examples of organizations with a service mission that have included advocacy as a major organizational goal and are actively involved in changing public policy. While more resource-intensive, combining services with advocacy can sometimes lead to a higher profile in the community and can translate into funding as well. The Henderson Mental Health Center in Fort Lauderdale, FL, raised awareness about mental illness by sponsoring a premiere viewing of the movie *Canvas* at a local theater in 2007. The actors and director were brought in to attend the viewing and give interviews to the local television and radio stations. As a result, the theater was packed and many new people became aware of Henderson; some also ultimately supported the organization financially.

A second method for establishing organizational expertise and credibility is through the sharing of knowledge and skills with others based on a competitive advantage. The simplest form of this is by building a database of statistics, reports, resources, publications, stories and more on a specific subject—ensuring that the press, public, researchers, and other interested parties contact that specific organization when needing information related to that area of specialty. Children at Risk in Houston, TX, is considered the premier source of data regarding local children's well-being thanks to their legislative reports, white papers, school rankings, and an annual publication called "Growing Up in Houston," which tracks several key indicators as diverse as environmental health and juvenile justice. Consequently, the press, funders, and even other grant professionals in the region trust this source of information more than those provided by official sources such as the Texas Education Agency's drop-out rates or the city of Houston's homeless population data.

On another level, Port Huron Hospital in Port Huron, MI, produces and broadcasts a television program called Today's Health featuring local physicians, health care specialists, and experts with the latest, most accurate information on current health care topics. Some YMCAs also present fitness- and health-related topics on local television and radio stations. Still other efforts are time specific: Mount Washington Observatory in North Conway, NH, recently conducted a summer series of lectures entitled "Science in the Mountains" with weekly topics focusing on climate change. Funded by foundations and other entities, the lectures were provided free to the public. Smaller nonprofits with limitations on resources or staff time may also engage in community advocacy, which consists of changing public opinion on a limited scope through presentations, conferences, or trainings on related issues. For example, several domestic violence agencies conduct trainings for police officers and health care professionals on how to recognize and deal with victims. Such trainings, although part of the mission, increase the public's image of these organizations as valuable resources in the community and provide the organizations the opportunity to offer outreach services to a larger audience.

While working in a specific area, program staff as well as grant profes- sionals may realize a gap in the community or a service area that requires attention on a larger scale than one organization can address. One way of dealing with such issues is by building collaborations with similar organiza- tions for the provision of services—this concept and its importance to funders is explained in Chapter 4. However, from a community image standpoint, one avenue of addressing service gaps or community needs is through community events and conferences. Some projects may be time- and locale-specific, such as the Maternity Care Coalition in Philadelphia, PA, attempting to address the region's childbirth crisis resulting from a rash of maternity unit closures by convening town hall meetings and making similar grassroots advocacy efforts. Other activities can be ongoing, such as quarterly or annual seminars bringing interested parties together to discuss what can be done about a certain issue.

Public relations can be a daunting task for those involved in grant seeking, and for many larger organizations there is often no need for interaction between the two areas. Many large entities have made concentrated efforts to interconnect departments and teams for specific tasks and purposes, although it is by no means a common occurrence. Smaller organizations have a slight advantage in that due to size and limited resources, grant professionals may be asked—even expected—to contribute in some way to the public relations effort. Regardless, by recognizing that this interaction is necessary in order to coordinate and streamline efforts for the benefit of the entire organization, staff and volunteers can embark on the path of improved branding, messaging, and ultimately more funding.

## Best Practice: The Rose

The Rose in Houston, TX, is a nonprofit providing breast cancer screening, diagnosis, and access to care to women through a network of health care providers and physicians offering pro-bono services. The logical next step from more than 20 years of collaborative efforts to increase access to breast healthcare in the Houston area was for The Rose to unite its informal health care provider network and bring together key stakeholders from breast cancer agencies throughout the state for the purpose of public discussion of issues. In 2005, the First Annual Breast Health Summit, co-sponsored by The Rose and the Susan G. Komen Breast Cancer Foundation Houston Affiliate, brought together more than 175 breast health care providers, physicians, social services agencies, community representatives, and survivors for a single purpose: to improve access to breast healthcare, particularly for low-income and uninsured clients. The summit was initially funded by a grant from the Centers for Disease Control. A presummit survey identified areas of greatest concern and created extraordinary interest in the event; the day ended with a list of objectives for future summits and 40 people responded to a "call to action" for planning the next summit. The summit was evaluated immediately and results disseminated through collaborators' websites and reports. The unique aspect of this summit series is that although many local conferences about breast cancer do exist, the Breast Health Summit is the only conference devoted to increasing access to care for the uninsured. Further, conference presenters are leaders and pioneers in the field of breast health and medicine. Interest and foundation funding has increased as the years have passed, and at the 4th Annual Breast Health Summit in 2008, a record-breaking attendance of 237 health care providers attended the day-long event. The success of the annual summits is best demonstrated by the creation of the Breast Health Collaborative of Texas, formalized in 2006 and now consisting of approximately 80 organizations from throughout Texas. Advocacy efforts of the Collaborative resulted in expanded Medicaid coverage for both screening and treatment, state-supported funding increased breast cancer screening by 20%, and National Treatment Funding doubled the number of women receiving treatment each month. As a direct result of these grassroots advocacy efforts, the National Breast Cancer Coalition Fund awarded the Collaborative its 2008 Best Practices in Breast Cancer Advocacy Award.

# Chapter 2 Checklist

## Organizational Readiness

| Indicator | Status |
|---|---|
| Does every staff and board member of our organization know and understand our mission statement? | |
| Do we conduct a strategic evaluation on a regular basis? | |
| Do our employee and volunteer evaluations include mission-specific goals and objectives? | |
| Are key stakeholders including clients, volunteers, and community leaders regularly contacted for advice and feedback? | |
| Do our public relations efforts include program-related activities aimed at improving community image? | |
| Is staff from programs and grants departments involved in public relations strategizing? | |
| Is our organization unified in branding and messaging across programs, locations, and departments? | |
| Do we have a crisis management plan and an audit committee? | |
| Do we adequately showcase the expertise of our employees and volunteers? | |
| Do we have access to credible community leaders or other people who will lend a positive community image to our organization? | |
| Do we conduct advocacy or knowledge-sharing activities aimed at establishing our organization's credibility and improving the sector as a whole? | |

## Grant Professional Readiness

| Indicator | Status |
|---|---|
| Do I have a clear understanding about my organization's mission and vision? | |
| Am I able to explain to funders how each of our programs aligns with our mission? | |
| Do I provide input to my leadership about funders' understanding of my organization's mission and programs? | |
| Am I involved in my organization's overall marketing and public relations activities? | |
| Do I work with marketing and programs staff to discuss funder-appropriate public relations activities? | |
| Do I keep track of the expertise and skills of our employees and volunteers and utilize them in my grant seeking efforts? | |
| Do I inform and educate my leadership about possible community-building, knowledge-sharing, and advocacy activities that may be important from a funder's perspective? | |

# Design Stellar Programs

> *"We are now trying to focus not on mission or programs but on the internal capacity to deliver services. This approach has allowed us to ask how one measures an organization's effectiveness, and identify its strengths and weaknesses, leading us to the continuum of life cycle of a highly effective organization. Although this is not new information, it typically is not applied to nonprofit organizations to measure effectiveness."*
>
> R. Andrew Swinney, President
> The Philadelphia Foundation

All nonprofit programs are not created equal. Program designs and methodologies run the gamut from the very simple to the highly complex and everything in between. Generally speaking, when an organization is in the initial stages of its life cycle, programs are either nonexistent or very simplistic. As it grows, it becomes more sophisticated in terms of market analysis, program design and delivery, and consequently funding. Grant professionals face different struggles depending on when they become involved with an organization and what their role is. In the absence of a grant professional, others in the organization—the founder, executive director, or board member—may be responsible for determining the need, methods and evaluation for specific programs. Nevertheless, organizations in varying stages of evolution and progress can make equal efforts in implementing and improving program aspects for the purpose of achieving long-term sustainability.

# Life Cycle Considerations

Very new organizations have the tremendous advantage of a clean slate, although few leaders and founders realize this. Hundreds of new nonprofits come into existence each year based on a need felt by an individual or group (one community may not have a sports outlet for at-risk youth, another may desperately need a community theater) yet many times there is no formal needs assessment or feasibility study to understand market realities. This assessment may take the form of informal focus groups and committee meetings, or more formalized feasibility studies; the aim is to understand whether a need exists, then to establish goals and objectives to achieve results. By seeking the advice of key stakeholders including prospective clients, a nonprofit can gather valuable information about individual and community needs, gaps in current services, and the best methods to provide new services. Some grant professionals may have access to start-up organizations because of their contributions as volunteers or even individual donors. Or they may have been requested to seek seed grants or start-up funds. These professionals can take advantage of their knowledge of foundation requirements and their understanding of the grant seeking process to encourage market analysis and business planning before pursuing grant opportunities. They can discuss program development with the appropriate staff or volunteers and ensure that some type of expertise in this area either exists or is brought in. An organization that begins its operations armed with such information has a much higher chance of success than one that assumes the need and creates programs based on presumptions rather than evidence.

Older organizations can also conduct feasibility studies to determine the market for their services by using a more business-like approach to planning. As detailed in an interview with Andrew Swinney, President of the Philadelphia Foundation, in Chapter 7, business planning tools can be used to understand internal strengths and weaknesses and to assess external threats and opportunities not only for program development but for the organization as a whole. For program development purposes, a business plan (1) is instrumental in comprehending community needs, analyzing costs to develop a new program or improve an existing one, and creating effective service delivery models. The results of the business planning process can also be used by grant professionals in their proposals or reports to funders; in fact, some organizations may be able to take a business plan to a foundation in order to convince them about the need to conduct more extensive research or for seed grants to launch a new program. In 2007, The OASIS Institute in St. Louis, MO, announced an ambitious five-year business plan to increase their impact through programs to reach a broader audience; the organization received initial funding from The Atlantic Philanthropies to develop the plan, and later $2.5 million over three years to implement it as well.

The Philadelphia Foundation explains that regardless of size and age, organizations that are highly effective in terms of mission impact have the following characteristics:

- Conducting comprehensive needs assessments using market research methods
- Documenting program models so that they become more transferable
- Developing a formal system for regularly evaluating programs
- Refining comprehensive programs based on changing needs
- Developing formal systems for integrating and using data from needs assessment, organizational assessment, program evaluation, and other sources, and using them for organizational improvement (2)

# Community Analysis

Many nonprofit staff and volunteers lose hope if told that extensive market analysis or needs assessment is necessary before launching operations. Alternatively, overworked program staff is often unwilling to embark on an examination of program design and delivery that will increase their work-load. While in some cases that may eventually have to happen, the reality is that for both new and established organizations, a wealth of resources may already exist that will help develop programs so that a lesser amount of work is needed for implementation and review.

The least work-intensive source of information is statistical data that shows need—crime, poverty levels, and other socioeconomic indicators available from a variety of sources including the U.S. Census and state and local government agencies. However, the danger in using this type of infor-mation is that it is extremely limited, may be several years old, and allows for presumptions about community need and service gaps. Other more reliable sources of information include the "lessons learned" shared by think tanks, large funders, and more established organizations in the field. For new organizations, these types of publications, meetings, or forums can provide a valuable impetus for providing services and learning about systems of delivery that work versus those that may not be as effective. By joining associations of similar organizations, or by becoming an affiliate of a national service agency, a nonprofit can benefit from information sharing, national studies, and the like. Girls Incorporated conducts studies and com-piles data on a variety of issues faced by girls, ranging from peer pressure to stereotypes in the media to science, math, and engineering career choices. Because much of this information is available on their website, organizations from a number of fields can access and make use of valid and reliable data for their own purposes.

Issue briefs, white papers, and other reports on specific topics can help nonprofits assess the need in their communities as well. Research findings, progress reports on programs, and outcome measurement data may be available through research organizations such as Public/Private Ventures, which has been instrumental in establishing needs assessments and evaluations for Big Brothers Big Sisters and Boys and Girls Clubs—more details on this topic will be given later in this chapter. Additionally, large entities sometimes conduct community research either for specific purposes or on an annual basis. The Community Research Institute (CRI), a joint venture of the Grand Rapids Community Foundation and Grand Valley State University, conducts extensive research to gather, analyze, and interpret data in a range of social, economic, and demographic conditions. CRI also conducts an annual community survey to obtain locally derived data that guides nonprofit leaders as they make decisions impacting their communities. Similarly, many United Way agencies assess the need in their communities and make the findings available to all interested parties. Other funders hold public meetings to gain community feedback and subsequently create reports or calls for action based on the data collected. Whether or not a nonprofit is a participant in this process, it can take advantage of the most recent local and regional findings from this most reliable of sources.

Program staff and even nonprofit leaders are often not in the best position to learn about the availability of these types of information. Grant professionals who network with each other as well as with funders can more easily assist program staff by researching and locating such reports and findings to bolster their program development efforts; ultimately, the same information can form key sections of the grant proposal as explained in Chapter 7.

After exhausting all possibilities, if an organization determines that the available resources are not sufficient to determine need or may not be enough to convince donors, conducting a specific needs assessment may become necessary. Both new and established nonprofits can hold community forums or conduct informal meetings with key constituents to understand issues and concerns and brainstorm possible solutions. Surveys, questionnaires, and other similar assessment techniques can also be employed depending upon the resources available.

Our research study showed that an overwhelming majority of respondents utilize some type of external references to justify the need for their programs (see Figure 3.1). Further, 69.2% of all respondents not presenting justification

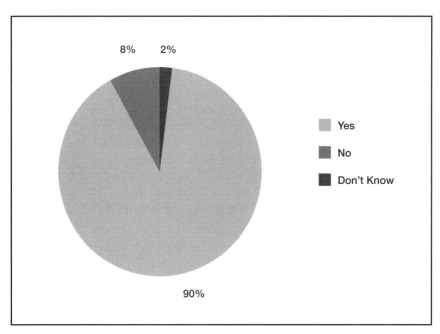

8%    2%

Yes

No

Don't Know

90%

Figure 3.1 *Use of External References to Justify Programs*

received less than 25% of funding from foundations. This data points to the fact that some smaller organizations but many more very large organizations are not accessing the power of community needs analysis to obtain higher levels of foundation funding.

Grant professionals should remember that funding is sometimes available for critical needs assessment projects. Many foundations and government agencies extend Request for Proposals for already identified needs, while others may be persuaded to fund such projects based on discussions with nonprofit leaders. The role of the grant professional in building bridges between nonprofit staff and funders to discuss these opportunities cannot be overemphasized. Although newer nonprofits may not find this a feasible strategy because of their lack of reputation in the community, older and well-known organizations considering a new program or service may easily hold the attention of local funders and attract a needs assessment grant. Going even further, funders and nonprofits may sometimes form collaborative efforts to research and solve community problems—see Chapter 10 for a detailed discussion on this form of collaboration.

Other low-cost methods of conducting community analysis include approaching experts in the research field for advice or assistance; apart from consultants and small research entities, this also includes a typically untapped resource: academic institutions. Universities and colleges often have community research departments that focus on serving nonprofit organizations in needs assessments and program evaluations; graduate or doctoral students of a particular department may also be willing to undertake smaller research projects as part of their coursework. The University of Houston's Graduate College of Social Work has a two pronged approach to community engagement—"faculty projects" where students are placed in local nonprofits for short term and ongoing assignments including needs assessments. This occurs through the Office of Community Projects, which includes a community-based research department. In 2008, partly through these efforts, the university received the Carnegie Foundation for the Advancement of Teaching's Tier 1 designation for community-engaged institutions—one of only 68 public institutions nationwide and the only public metropolitan university in Texas with the classification.

If resources are limited or if the required level of expertise is not available within one organization, formal or informal nonprofit collaborations may be created to assess community needs in a certain neighborhood or area. There are many benefits to this type of project: a larger cross section of the population can be surveyed using the clients, constituents, or key advisors of each partner, and the results can offer value to all collaborators within their own spheres of service.

Regardless of method and scope, community analysis and information gathering should continue on an ongoing basis. This is another important role grant professionals can play in the overall success of the organization. At the very least, reports and statistics already available within the community should be monitored frequently to ensure that grant proposals and programs are both benefitting from updated data and new studies by third parties. Program staff can be reminded quarterly or annually to submit their ideas for new programs or projects so that timely research and needs assessment can be conducted without the pressure of deadlines.

# Program Design

Once the needs and issues facing the community and target audience have been understood, program goals and objectives can be more easily determined. Again, an interdepartmental team approach is the best method of ensuring that all ideas are taken into account and funder expectations are built into the program design from the beginning. Although the complexities of program development are beyond the scope of this book (3), it is important to note that some elements should be considered not only because of their value to a well-functioning program, but also for purposes of inclusion in grant proposals. In a team environment consisting of program leaders, front line staff, marketing and accounting staff, as well as grant professionals, the following issues should be considered at length:

- Goals: what are the goals of the proposed program, and how do they fit within the overall organizational goals and mission? Are there possibilities of conflict with existing programs? Why is the program important— sufficient needs assessment is necessary before the team should move forward to the next steps.

- Target Audience: who will be served, and what are their demographics? Are they already served by other programs within the organization, or is an entirely new population being targeted? What are the special needs of the people being served? How will they be recruited?

- Action Plan: what type of strategies or activities can be devised to achieve the goals of the program? Will a specific curriculum or delivery method by followed, and if so, from where will it be derived? What are the inputs and outputs? What is the timeline for each activity and for the program as a whole? Note that timelines should be comprehensive and include marketing, public relations, and grant application, as well as timelines for program activities. Further, each activity in the timeline should have responsible persons assigned to it and deadlines for assignments to be completed.

- Key Personnel: who will be involved in each step of the action plan? What will their scope of services be? Will they need training? Will interdepartmental cooperation be required? Will additional staff need to be hired, and if so, how and when will this be achieved? This discussion should allow for collaborative partners and their competencies; therefore, advisors and collaborators may be included in some or all meetings as well.

- Volunteers: how will volunteers be used within the program? Is their role necessary for program success, or are they being included merely for public relations purposes? What activities will be performed for volunteer recruitment, training, management, and recognition? These should also be included in the timeline above.

- Evaluation: how will the program be documented and assessed? What are the objectives, and how will success be measured? What tools will be used for outcome measurement? Who will be responsible for evaluation? More importantly, how will the information gathered be used for program revisions and improvements? Evaluations are discussed in more detail later in this chapter.

- Resource Allocation: what materials and supplies will you require for program activities—including marketing the program—and what is their estimated cost? Which of these may possibly be funded by outside sources? Are some or all resources available in-house to be shared within programs or departments? Are there possibilities for earning income such as program fees, and if so, how should prices be determined? Are there possibilities for in-kind donations or sharing of resources from other organizations? What will evaluation cost? Remember to include staffing and technology concerns in this discussion.

In many organizations, grant professionals are not included in this type of planning process, even though they can be instrumental in many aspects. They can help program and management staff understand the distinction between in-house and externally-created methodologies and determine which option is the best fit based on overall strategic plans and available resources. They are also in an ideal position to discuss resource allocation—how staff, technology, and funds will be needed and where they will be derived from. Although it is expected that program leaders will already have working knowledge of terminology such as goals, objectives, inputs, and outcomes, many times these issues are not clarified in the initial phases of program design and development. As a result, many new programs are created without proper regard for such factors. Grant professionals, if involved in the planning stages, can remind staff about the importance of written goals and objectives and appropriate dissemination to all concerned. They can assist in working through the logistics of a proposed program, such as service delivery methods, possible collaborations, and timelines. Additionally, grant professionals can suggest ways to improve the program design based on funder requirements, such as creating advisory panels, building in time for guest speakers, incorporating corporate volunteering, and considering opportunities for earned income.

As mentioned above, an interdepartmental approach to program planning can help identify many potential problems and ensure the success of the program. While program staff typically have the most knowledge about programs, they may need to work with grant professionals when creating budgets in order to identify funder red flags, such as high administrative to program cost ratios and inflated or unjustified expense increases from one year to the next. More importantly, the accounting or finance department should be involved in program planning in order to determine which resources are already available and which ones will need to be funded. Similarly, marketing staff should also provide input in program development in order to determine how to publicize a new program to clients, volunteers, and funders. Another stakeholder category that will benefit from being involved in the planning process is board leadership; as explained in Chapters 1 and 2, a higher level of leadership engagement results from a thorough understanding of an organization's mission, vision, and programs.

Program methodologies differ from one organization to another; some are based on curriculum created in-house by staff or consultants, while others use methodologies created by experts in the field. Still other nonprofits use program methods conceived by staff, volunteers, or even clients. Roca in Chelsea, MA, uses Prochaska's Stages of Change in their programs, while People's Grocery's "Peer 2 Peer" program was created by interns and other youth involved in the organization. Countless youth organizations, including the YMCA, use the Search Institute's framework of Developmental Assets to develop their programs. Our study asked respondents about the use of established curriculum and methodologies and discovered a split: 47.1% of organizations reported using such methodologies while 42.5% replied in the negative (see Figure 3.2). Budget size also seemed to determine this aspect of programming: of those who did use established methodologies, more than half of respondents (52.8%) were *very large budget* organizations, while 18.1% were *small budget* (see Figure 3.3).

Linking back to community analysis, 93% of organizations using some type of program methodology also justified their programs with the help of statistics, data, and other relevant studies. It seems as if the use of both goes hand in hand—or at least an awareness of one may lead to recognition of the importance of the other.

When designing a new program, an organization should try to utilize existing methodologies because of their proven success; if an entirely new or little

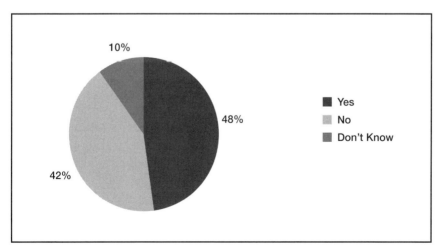

Figure 3.2 *Use of Established Curriculum or Methodologies in Programs*

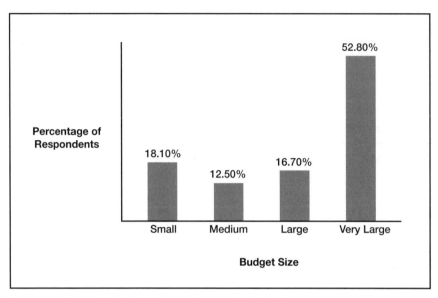

Figure 3.3 *Use of Methodology or Curriculum by Size*

known methodology is being used, it may be feasible to conduct a pilot program on a small scale to test it and determine the possibility of success. Some non-profits prefer to work with experts to design and develop their own curriculum. OASIS does so for a multitude of programs and courses: their "Free from Fall" curriculum was created with the help of researchers at the Fall Prevention Center of Excellence in Los Angeles, while "Living a Healthy Life," focusing on chronic health conditions, was developed at Stanford University.

## Best Practice: Wellspring House

Wellspring House in Gloucester, MA, began in 1981 as a shelter for homeless families. Ten years later, in 1990, a research project by the organization interviewed more than 80 former shelter guests to find out where they were in their lives and what had happened to them since moving into their own homes. The research, published under the title "We Are Like You," was studied and discussed at a two-day symposium in 1991; as a result of working groups started at that symposium, Wellspring began developing extensive education programs for low-income women to help them prepare for jobs that pay a living wage, as well as family education programs to help strengthen and improve family interaction.

Programs, once designed, should be documented in order to ensure that they can be reproduced by new staff members and replicated by other organizations or at other locations if needed. Although this may be done in the form of a manual, it is better to give programs a visual form so that they can be easily understood by everyone. Logic models, flow charts, diagrams, and other types of visual representations of program design are very effective in not only communicating internally but also externally to volunteers, clients, and the general public. Additionally, grant professionals find it much easier to communicate a new program to potential funders if the design and service delivery is explained in the form of a picture or table that can be used in conjunction with verbal and written discussions. The diagrams may refer to an entire service delivery model or to specific processes, such as steps in training or case management.

## Measuring Success

Funders of all types look at evaluation plans as a key factor in successful program design. Most grant applications and funder guidelines ask questions about outcome measurement, and a majority of grant professionals do understand the importance of including objectives in their proposals and describing ways to measure success based on the objectives. However, many times they are hindered by program staff—especially those serving in the trenches—who view evaluation as an annoyance increasing their work load without serving a real purpose. In other cases, evaluation plans are created specifically for proposals or to fulfill various reporting requirements, which results in a lack of motivation to collect data during the year and inaccurate or incomplete information at year-end.

Although most organizations receiving grants or private donations understand that they are accountable to donors, stakeholders, and even to the general public, there is hesitancy in measuring outcomes or reporting success unless required by a grant contract or other means. Many nonprofits consider it sufficient to count the number of clients served at year end, without regard to how that service compares to previous years in number or quality. In other organizations, there is a bias of qualitative over quantitative data, or vice versa. The reality is that in order to be truly accountable, an organization should not only measure its efficiency but also its effectiveness, and both these issues should be raised during strategic planning and program design, rather than when a proposal is bring submitted. A host of literature exists on the topic of outcome measurement—from the creation of logic models to technical data collection methods—and each organization must determine the right measurement techniques for itself (3). Grant professionals who are involved in program design or are at least part of the discussions can ensure that an evaluation plan is created for the organization as a whole, as well as for individual programs and projects as described earlier in this chapter. When that happens, the likelihood will increase that the data collected is timely, valuable, and can be used not only for reporting purposes but also for internal improvements.

In itself, outcome measurement that leads to program and organizational improvements—including betterment of staff—should be cause for celebration for nonprofit leaders and program directors. Even if none of the organization's funders require reports at the end of a grant, setting objectives and measuring success will ultimately lead to a better understanding of whether a program, service delivery model, or component is working. Even with very simplistic evaluation plans, such as feedback forms or pre- and post-testing, the aim should be to understand (a) whether the program is working, and (b) whether the client is satisfied. If either of these two questions is left unanswered at the end of the program or project, then adjustments should be made. Within this broad definition, many smaller questions, known as outcomes, may be created based on what the organization is hoping to accomplish. Again, it is advisable to conduct such planning activities as a team effort, including not only program staff but also grant professionals, public relations staff, and others within the organization. Grant professionals often have detailed knowledge of the types of outcomes funders may be interested in measuring and can therefore help guide the process by bringing to light the preferences of major local funders. Or, at the very least, they know the foundations that are currently supporting the organization, so that these requirements can be built into the program design if possible. They can also seek funder input on specific evaluation plans for the organization's industry or ask to be connected to experts who may be of assistance in designing or conducting evaluations if needed.

Important issues to address in the early stages of evaluation development from a grant professional's perspective are:

- What are the objectives of the program? Discuss the inclusion of numbers as well as percentage increases or decreases. Roca uses an extensive outcome measurement system to measure not only economic independence of youth involved in the problem—employment and education—but also engagement outcomes based on the Transitional Relationship model used by the agency. Also important are soft outcomes such as satisfaction rates and psychologic indicators; many organizations providing health services track patient satisfaction levels with not only the treatment but also quality of care provided by health professionals. Client stories, testimonials, and quotes should also be collected, especially if the program or service in question is new or may not have sufficient support from funders.

- Who will be assessed? In addition to clients, many nonprofits track volunteer performance as a means of showing the need for their particular brand of service delivery; for instance, I Have a Dream Houston measures the level of satisfaction that Dreamers (clients) have with their Dream Partners (volunteer mentors) by assessing criteria such as "I trust my Dream Partner with my secrets and private feelings." Organizations that deal extensively with community partners also track partner performance and satisfaction levels, such as the Capital Area Food Bank in Washington, DC, whose "agency relations" indicators include the number of clients helped by member agencies and the number of agency compliance visits completed. In order to assess efficiency, the food bank also tracks the cost of supplies and food.

- How will data be collected and by whom? Grant professionals should know who is responsible for collecting and managing data and should have access to outcome information so that reports to funders can be prepared in a timely manner. Further, a thorough analysis of resources—staff and technology being foremost—is necessary to ensure that the evaluation plan can actually be implemented. Some nonprofits use paper surveys and Excel files to gather and analyze data, while others use expensive software systems that require training and maintenance. The best type of outcome measurement is one that becomes a regular element of program activities, rather than an added responsibility for staff or volunteers, for example by incorporating data collection into daily client intake and tracking.

- How will shortfalls be tracked and rectified? Frequent reviews can be implemented by program staff and grant professionals to review progress against goals and objectives. Instead of relying on annual results, quarterly milestones can be established for internal purposes. Results of shortfalls or negative outcomes should be discussed in light of reporting to funders, but more importantly to analyze program inefficiencies in order to make improvements in service delivery. Only when ongoing discussions are the norm within an organization, program staff will not feel threatened and will be more likely to come forward with disappointing results in a timely manner.

- How will the results be used? This should include discussions with grant professionals, marketing staff, collaborating agencies, and other stakeholders to ensure that a variety of data relevant to all is being gathered. A further discussion of outcome tracking and dissemination techniques is included in Chapter 9.

# Funder Perspective: Weingart Foundation
*Jill Seltzer, Former Program Officer*

Q: What is the value of outcome measurement to a grantee as well as to your foundation?

A: In the case of foundation trustees sitting around a table making joint decisions, they are looking for proposals that make a convincing case that grant dollars are going to accomplish something. And that argument is clearly made through outcome measurements. On the other hand, through outcome measurements, grantees are able to refer to the original program objectives and honestly report what "came true" and what changed because that's how life is. We hope that whatever is measured is of value to the nonprofit itself. Organizations should realize the value of outcome measurements because we all want to know that what we are doing matters. The outcomes provide a level of accountability and evidence that the program has not been an exercise on futility.

Q: Are there any examples of "bad" or "ineffective" outcomes that non-profits should avoid?

A: For example, "improve students' self-esteem" is not a very effective outcome because how exactly can you measure self-esteem and whether it has in fact improved? It is better to measure increased attendance or parent involvement. Here's a specific example from a grant we made recently to a neighborhood center, which wanted to measure whether or not their street worker intervention was actually stemming violence. When the police think that trouble is brewing, they call the center and ask them to send their street workers to intervene. When they make that call, they write up the event they hope they're preventing with all the particulars: time, place, players, what they hope to prevent. A week later, the police revisit that report and add more information such as, did it break out in violence or not? The good news for the center is that this results in some tangible evidence when their intervention prevented something from happening, and not just because they said so. . .the police are saying so.

Q: Are there any preferred methods of evaluation, and if so, why are they superior to others?

A: Actually, assessment is a viable alternative because it's more realistic and subjective and often more affordable. And often an internal, built-in assessment means that the nonprofit takes the time to reflect on its programs and apply lessons learned to future program design.

Program design and development can be a complicated task, and many grant professionals may enter an organization too late to impact it. By discussing the needs of the grants department at every turn and reminding leadership and staff that outcome measurement is crucial to the success of the organization, grant professionals can ensure that their grant seeking strategy is more successful than ever before.

## ENDNOTES

(1) See List of Suggested Resources.
(2) "Characteristics of High Performing Nonprofits" The Philadelphia Foundation www.philafound.org/Portals/0/Uploads/Documents/Public/High_Performance_ Standards_for_Nonprofit_Orgs.pdf
(3) See List of Suggested Resources.

# Chapter 3 Checklist

## Organizational Readiness

| Indicator | Status |
|---|---|
| Are we aware of community needs and issues, and do our programs reflect current service gaps? | |
| Do we conduct periodic business planning to assess internal strengths and weaknesses and to understand external threats and opportunities? | |
| Does program design and development occur in a team environment involving not only program staff but also marketing, grants, and finance departments? | |
| Do we use established methodologies for our programs? | |
| Do we have an evaluation system in place for periodic review of programs, measurement of key outcomes, and for future improvements? | |
| Does program staff understand the value of outcome measurement and data collection, and are these elements part of their daily responsibilities? | |

# Grant Professional Readiness

| Indicator | Status |
|---|---|
| Do I utilize community needs assessments to convince funders of the value of my organization? | |
| Do I regularly network with other grant professionals and funders to understand emergent community issues and provide feedback to my leadership? | |
| Am I able to bring my leadership together with funders and other community partners to discuss opportunities for community assessment or analysis? | |
| Do I monitor current data and statistics in order to alert my leadership, staff, and outside agencies such as funders for the need for new analysis? | |
| Do I work with program staff and senior leadership to help design and develop programs? | |
| Do I have working knowledge of program components, service delivery methods, and evaluation systems used by my organization? | |
| Do I work with program staff to collect outcome data, client stories, and testimonials on a regularly established schedule? | |

# Unite and Do Good

*"When more than one agency focuses on an issue, it increases the likelihood of addressing and finding service gaps. Agencies serve the same people in different aspects, and if they are collaborating, they are more likely to identify where services are missing."*

Kevin Cain, President and CEO
The John Rex Endowment

Several decades ago, collaborations between nonprofits were few and far between. In recent years, more and more nonprofits are admitting to the impossibility of solving growing community needs by themselves and recognizing the value of sharing resources across organizations to expand the scope of services. Although typically a program role, collaborations can benefit from the input and experience of grant professionals, as these individuals continue to become a valuable part of collaborative committees and work groups.

## Why Collaborate?

Partnerships come in many forms and for many reasons, although all do not ultimately result in program success. The mindset in prior years was for nonprofits to work in isolation and only approach other organizations when a funding opportunity presented itself. Unfortunately, partnerships that come into existence due to a grant opportunity are typically the weakest type of relationship; since they are based on the short-sighted goal of receiving funding, the chances of long-term program success are limited. This happens because the goals and objectives of the partnership—and the resulting project—are based not on organizational mission and goals but on funder priorities. Although in some cases these types of partnerships may go on to become long-lasting relationships, too often they fall apart after the grant period is finished. Many times, it is the grant professional who is responsible for bringing partners together for the purposes of a grant application; care must be taken to assess the real reasons for working together and to weigh the costs and benefits before moving forward. A team approach that offers suggestions from program staff as well as key stakeholders such as volunteers and clients can be very valuable in determining whether a potential partnership is indeed mission-centric.

Certain collaborations are formed in order to conduct research or provide information on a regular basis not just to the partners but to other organizations as well. The Asset Builders Alliance in Cincinnati, OH, a collaboration of local youth serving agencies, was founded by the YMCA of Greater Cincinnati, the Boys and Girls Clubs of Greater Cincinnati, the Boy Scouts—Dan Beard Council, and the Girl Scouts of Western Ohio, and funded by the United Way of Greater Cincinnati. With the mission of mobilizing and engaging the community around the Search Institute's Developmental Asset research, the alliance offers trainings and networking opportunities around this model. Additionally, in 2007 they administered a regional survey of 7th and 11th graders to create a baseline of key areas that can be used by other organizations, policy makers, and educators. While many nonprofits across the country use the Developmental Asset model, localized current research on how local youth behave, what they consider important, and how they measure against the nation's youth is infinitely more valuable from a community assessment and program delivery standpoint.

Typically, program-specific partnerships—those that are created around the individual agencies' program designs—have a greater chance of achieving positive results. The aim then becomes to serve a common purpose, perhaps with the intention of reaching a larger number of clients or taking advantage of expertise available in one organization but not in the other. A nonprofit teaching financial literacy to students may partner with a college to utilize the skills and knowledge of its professors, while several arts organizations may band together to conduct joint activities. On the other hand, many organizations serving at-risk youth prefer to build relationships with schools in order to provide after-school programming, mentoring activities, leadership training, and substance abuse prevention to their student population. The schools realize that although the need exists for such programs and activities, they themselves do not have the expertise—nor is it aligned with their mission—to provide such services. They are more than willing to bring in external sources in the form of community organizations with expertise in specific areas for this very purpose; the resulting collaboration is a one-to-many relationship between each school and its partners. Nonprofits with this type of community model therefore have limited or no brick-and-mortar existence, preferring to work with partners such as schools to offer their specialized programming in the field. Communities in Schools is an example of such a model: they not only provide services directly on school campuses but also connect students with other resources by partnering with third party nonprofits to offer specialized services they themselves cannot provide. Such a complex collaborative community model requires a high level of relationship management and technical support in order to ensure that all partners are dedicated and able to conduct the overall program.

## Best Practice: OASIS Houston

When OASIS Houston began making plans to offer the nationally acclaimed "Active Living" everyday curriculum to Houston-area seniors in 2003, it was determined by leadership and potential funders that the program should be expanded beyond the original pilot. Program staff contacted several community organizations already serving seniors and put together a meeting to determine interest. The OASIS programs head was brought in from their headquarters in St. Louis, MO, to explain the "Active Living" curriculum and go over the research. The staff then developed a coalition of organizations, taught the program to them, and trained people to facilitate and conduct the program; the entire preparation and training process spanned almost a year. OASIS Houston developed the entire plan with the premise that they would no longer remain a hands-on agency but rather would empower partner agencies to implement the program and reach more seniors. Partners were selected by looking at their diverse audiences to whom OASIS Houston was not already providing services, such as Hispanics or those located in zip codes determined to be below poverty levels by the federal government. They also tried to identify organizations with similar missions to OASIS; during the one-year process, some partners were lost because their mission or their activities changed from what OASIS considered important. The partner agencies were assigned responsibilities such as providing space for the 20-week program, publicizing the program within their communities, and training a staff member. It was found that agencies that were able to identify a staff member to train and liaison with OASIS Houston moved forward more quickly into the program; it was also realized early on that partners were in the unique position to find the right facilitator. Therefore, OASIS Houston made every effort to provide support and assistance to partners, such as a five-page detailed list of what to look for in a facilitator. The resulting 22-member coalition called the Houston Healthy Lives Coalition recently received the United States Administration on Aging's Program Champion Award.

Many other organizations keep programs separate but work together for advocacy purposes. Consider again The Rose's Breast Health Collaborative mentioned in Chapter 3: a major contribution of the Collaborative is its efforts on behalf of the Breast Health Resource Mapping Project, an interactive, online map mapping project initially developed by St. Luke's Episcopal Health Charities in Houston, TX. Several Collaborative partners serve on the project's data committee; plans are underway to take over the project and eventually cover all 57 Texas counties. As a direct result of these grassroots advocacy efforts, the Collaborative won the 2008 Best Practices in Breast Cancer Advocacy Award and $50,000 from the National Breast Cancer Coalition Fund.

The same type of non-programmatic partnership can be built around marketing activities as well: several years ago, leaders from arts and cultural institutions in the Phoenix area came together to discuss their marketing and ticketing concerns. With support from the Arizona Commission on the Arts, more than two years was invested in research and deliberation through a "Ticketing Tactics Task Force," fondly known among organizations' marketing staff as "TicTacs." This task force, with support from a local foundation, presented an action plan to attract new audiences through the creation of Alliance for Audience, a nonprofit collaborative effort of more than a hundred arts organizations addressing the scarcity of marketing resources and discussing the development of new ticketing technologies, including a joint website called ShowUp.com. This and other types of collaborative efforts enhance the credibility of the group in a way not possible for any single organization and lead to improved relationships with funders and the public.

In uncertain economic conditions, many organizations find creative and long-lasting ways to collaborate, not programmatically but administratively. In order to cut costs without sacrificing the quality and reach of social services, nonprofits may decide to share facilities or to combine back office operations such as software systems and databases, billing, human resources, and the like.

If needed and appropriate, mergers can also sometimes be a viable option for sharing resources and increasing the reach of partner organizations by taking advantage of complementary expertise; however, it should be mentioned that mergers and acquisitions are not considered by some experts as collaborative efforts since they usually lead to relinquished autonomy by one or more partners. In any event, one notable merger in recent years is The Museum of Nature & Science in Dallas—the result of a 2006 combining of three cultural institutions: the Dallas Museum of Natural History, The Science Place, and the Dallas Children's Museum. Although the merger faced challenges related to the integration of technical systems and

---

## Best Practice: MACC CommonWealth

The MACC CommonWealth in Minneapolis, MN, has created an innovative model for administrative efficiency for the Twin Cities' nonprofit sector. Launched on January 1, 2007, as a joint venture among five human service providers—Family & Children's Service, MACC Alliance of Connected Communities, Phyllis Wheatley Community Center, Pillsbury United Communities, and Plymouth Christian Youth Center—the Commonwealth's services include Finance (accounting, reporting, Form 990, audit support, cash management), Human Resources (benefits, performance review, staff support), and Information Technology (client data system management, help desks, networking and internet access). As a result, member agencies have saved approximately $200,000 in the first year of operations alone, translating to an additional 1,000 clients. Resources used to provide services to member agencies are owned by MACC CommonWealth, and agencies are charged for services according to the proportion of resources they utilize. The CommonWealth staff is accountable to a Board of Governors; each member organization has two seats on the Board. In recognition of the valuable collaborative and resource savings performed by the organization, Lodestar Foundation, in association with the Arizona-Indiana-Michigan Alliance, named the CommonWealth one of 30 semifinalists for its 2008 "Collaboration Prize."

---

organizational cultures, the benefits of expanded and improved programming and exhibits and the reduction of duplicate staff efforts has resulted in higher attendance by the public as well as increased funding. In Sylvania, OH, the YMCA and the United Jewish Council of Greater Toledo merged despite resistance from several forces in order to save administrative costs and the expenses related to building a new facility for the Y. Although funders were initially wary of the merger because of opposing missions and competing programs, the resulting benefits have included an increased donor pool and a better understanding of Christian and Jewish faiths in the community.

Not all nonprofits collaborate, of course. In our study, however, it was discovered that a majority of respondents collaborated with other organizations, while some prefer to work in isolation (see Figure 4.1). Of the ones that do collaborate, an equal number were *small budget* (23.9%) and *large budget* (23%); however, the largest number of collaborators lay in the *very large*

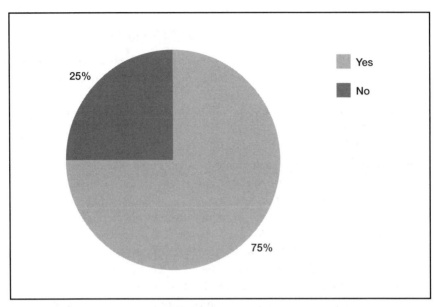

Figure 4.1 *Collaborations with Other Nonprofits*

*budget* category (44.2%). Perhaps this is a result of having better resources at their disposal for the proper implementation and follow up of partner agency activities (see Figure 4.2).

Grant professionals who discuss organizational issues and challenges with their colleagues on a regular basis can bring potential partners together for open discussions. More than anyone else, they can keep their ears open for training and funding opportunities from foundations regarding these strategic partnerships and alert nonprofit leadership about the benefits of cost sharing activities. Funding possibilities for collaborative efforts range from grant funds for joint programs to paying for technical assistance and consultant fees. From funders' perspective, collaborations are a powerful tool for serving more people in the community and pooling resources for the best possible results. However, they also recognize that all collaborations are not destined for spectacular results. Most funders know that partnering on superficial issues is not as valuable as coming together to solve deep-rooted problems; examples abound of nonprofits successfully working together in the communities they serve, but even more instances of failed partnerships exist. For this and other reasons, leaders of partnering organizations may find it helpful to discuss their ideas and plans for collaborations with program officers before moving forward with time- or grant-specific partnerships.

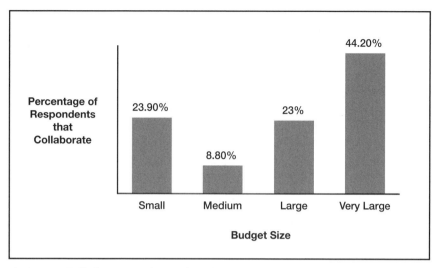

Figure 4.2 *Collaborations by Budget Size*

# Planning for Collaboration

The basic ingredients of a successful partnership or strategic alliance are committed leadership and face-to-face communications with each other on a fairly regular basis. These two elements improve trust and understanding between partnering agencies and their staff and force potential problems to the forefront while they are still manageable. The steps to building and sustaining a successful partnership may be explained through an analysis of the Westside Infant Network (WIN), a virtual entity that exists among a coalition of three primary social service nonprofits in Los Angeles, CA. The key to success is to conduct planning and evaluation for partnering activities similar to what occurs for program activities. The best time to explore possible collaborations is before a program or project has begun, so that the collaborating agencies' staff and leadership, including grant professionals, can participate in the discussions about program design and development. The main questions to ask each other in this initial stage are:

- Why is there a need to partner? This includes a discussion of common mission, interests, and needs from a staff and leadership perspective; organizations that plan for collaborations from the highest level down have a clearer vision of what is to be achieved through the partnership. In the case of WIN, discussions within the local nonprofit community led to the discovery that several organizations were seeing clients demonstrating symptoms of infant

## Funder Perspective: The John Rex Endowment
*Kevin Cain, President and CEO*

Q: Why are collaborations important to your foundation and to most foundations in general?

A: We don't require collaborations on our grants; in fact, many of our grants are from a single organization's proposal. Although I think we will continue this, the longer we are working in this field the more appealing collaborations are becoming. Collaborations shifts the focus of "we want to do more of the same" to "we've got an idea for a new or improved way to meet needs"—that's more appealing to me as a funder.

Q: How do you suggest nonprofits begin collaborative efforts?

A: Collaborations acknowledge that different agencies have different expertise and knowledge. Rather than one agency doing everything, there is a realization that they know who else to bring to the table. As a local funder, we see a lot of small agencies that honestly don't have the expertise to be doing what they promise to do in their proposals. It's essential to come talk to us first—have a conversation face-to-face and explain who's in charge, who's making decisions, and who's responsible for what. Memorandums of Understanding (MOUs) are important, but the conversation is even more important because we talk about roles and responsibilities. Letters of support on the other hand have no value to me because there is no commitment. Usually I don't even consider them when looking at a proposal. There should be very clear expectations as a participating agency; the level of detail and commitment up front is very important so that you don't get caught up in these issues later and can focus on implementation. Agencies should do the homework about service gaps, local service delivery systems, and community needs before approaching us. Money is so scarce that to avoid duplication of services, it is important for us to hear of a service that isn't already being provided.

Q: Can funders play a role in encouraging collaborations in the community?

A: As local funders, we can sometimes connect agencies together if we feel there is a potential for collaboration. We recently awarded a grant to a medical center that identifies kids with risk factors for Type 2 diabetes and offers intervention programs. Someone came to us afterwards seeking a grant for a summer camp for the same population and similar programs. We felt that they should connect with the medical expertise that the medical center possesses. However, if that collaboration happens, we will look for evidence of that connection by for example reviewing the protocol, etc. But of course that takes time and effort. . .it's always much more productive and positive to have conversations that are not dictated by a proposal deadline.

mental health (IMH) issues; however, since this field is fairly new, none had specific expertise to serve these clients. With the financial and technical support of the Atlas Family Foundation, six organizations decided to collaborate around the area of children's mental health, even though it serves a small intersection of the collaborating agencies' client base.

- What is the collaboration plan? Similar to program development, this line of discussion should include the what, when, where, and how of the actual provision of services through the partnership. Each partner agency within WIN offers a special set of services that cannot be offered by the other agencies, such as health clinic services by one, homeless services and job training by another, and early care and school readiness services by a third. Each agency has its own staff and programs, and for their WIN clients (those needing IMH services), agencies provide intensive, shared case management underwritten by WIN. The agency case managers provide basic support, while WIN therapists, who are Master's level professionals, provide in-home dyadic therapy, working hand-in-hand with agency case managers to ensure that both basic and therapeutic services are well-coordinated across agencies. Further, a web-based HIPAA-compliant communications network allows each partner to not only share information and services for families they are serving in collaboration, but also to view the work at other departments and agencies. This ensures that everyone who needs to have access to a patient's records has the most up-to-date information. It also encourages the sharing of knowledge and data across diverse organizations.

- What will each partner bring to the table? If partners are included in the planning process mentioned earlier in this chapter, they will be more committed to the program's success. Further, many individual agency limitations will be revealed during the planning phase, and the decision can be made relatively early on whether to proceed or not based on the strengths and weaknesses of the potential partners. Since nonprofits, not unlike other business entities, have differing levels of human and technical capacity, it is also important to know before entering into an agreement how various staffing and technical issues will be handled during the course of program delivery. Not only can levels of expertise and skill differ, but program-related benchmarks such as operational and case management standards can differ as well. WIN realized the need for a standard of care agreed upon by each partner in order to ensure consistency and quality, so that each client receives the same care and case management regardless of which partner agency provides the service. As a result, three of the six partner agencies moved to a lower level of partnership, so that although they do not receive grant funds raised by the coalition, they have access to trainings and other program benefits.

- How will the partners communicate? Regularly scheduled interagency staff meetings are an important factor in WIN's success. At the highest level, the executive directors meet monthly to review the WIN budget and discuss major policy issues. The program committee also meets monthly to discuss implementation issues and challenges. Thirdly, case managers meet on a weekly basis to review specific cases based on a specific case review schedule. At each meeting, five clients/families are reviewed, and all case managers involved in those cases appear at the meetings. However, less intensive collaborations can use email or quarterly meetings to discuss issues and solve arising problems.

- How will the performance of the collaboration be measured? Certain tools such as the Internal Collaborative Functioning Scales (1) can be used to gauge the workings of any partnership. Outcome measurement can also be built into program evaluation plans: using survey results to assess partner satisfaction, for example. At WIN, not only are client evaluations such as standardized screenings and testing utilized for assessing program achievements, but case managers are also evaluated monthly using 10 performance benchmarks.

- How will resources, including funding, be allocated? Since WIN conducts fundraising activities to raise money for all partners as well as to support its in-house budget, fund allocations are tied to performance benchmarks, resulting in higher case management performance across the coalition. Additionally, WIN's Executive Director compiles a fundraising report each month for the other coalition leaders; this allows for transparency and collaborations in fundraising, sometimes resulting in joint grant applications among partners.

As touched upon in the above analysis, measuring the success of the collaboration is important for the overall success of the programs operating under it. For nonprofits starting the planning process, setting outcomes related to the objectives of the partnership as well as on partner feedback can be very beneficial. MOUs, contracts, and other similar documents are useful tools for taking partnerships from concept to reality; the more detailed these documents, the higher the chances of success due to accountability. Wraparound Oregon uses an Interagency Agreement that defines not only collaborative goals but also each partner's specific responsibilities from the very basic, such as participating in committee meetings and providing staff members, down to the details, such as allowing for the use of computers and office supplies as needed. This four-page agreement, signed by partner agency representatives, also explains the process of solving disputes and disagreements between parties.

Individual agency outcomes may also include collaborative outcomes as a way to measure overall effectiveness and show funders their level of commitment to the collaborative effort. Many nonprofits ask partners to complete feedback forms as part of their program evaluation, so that challenges faced during the year can be addressed and the partnership effort can be improved in the future. Objectives may range from "90% of current partners will express a high degree of satisfaction with their experience" to "All old partnerships will be maintained in the current year and two new collaborations with schools or community centers will be established in the following year."

## Acquiring Financial Support

Grant professionals submitting proposals based on collaborating efforts must ensure that funders' questions about the sustainability of the union are satisfactorily answered—most of these answers will need to be carefully researched and discussed with program and fundraising management. They also should be prepared to fully understand and communicate the joint benefits of a partnership as they relate to client outcomes or other key success measures: for example serving more people, providing additional services to the same population, saving operating expenses by eliminating waste, or increasing training opportunities for volunteers and staff. Another reality to be aware of is that grant proposals for joint programs may also suffer from decreased funding in some cases; often a foundation may decide to grant a lower amount to two agencies combined, rather than larger, separate amounts.

However, in long-term partnerships such as those described in this chapter, grant professionals have the opportunity to work closely with their counterparts at other organizations and take advantage of complementing skills, expertise, and funder relationships for superior grant proposals. Rather than compete for grants, they can create joint proposals and seek funding from foundations that may not be within the reach of individual organizations; for example, many large foundations require that potential grantees serve a larger geographic area or even be national in scope. WIN was able to apply for and receive funding from various foundations including the Robert Wood Johnson Foundation's Local Funding Partnership in 2007 due to their collaborative model. The organization was also featured in 2008 in a study by the W.K. Kellogg Foundation as one of eight exemplary programs using innovation and collaboration to serve children.

The staff of other departments, such as public relations and marketing, can also work together for joint publicity activities, especially to raise the profile of the partner agencies at the time that collaboration begins or when accomplishments occur. Needless to say, the community image of the partners may improve or diminish as a result of the partnership, so prior discussions in this regard are necessary to ensure a smooth public relations effort. By detailed planning and through dedicated focus on the mission of the organizations, the purpose of collaboration can be achieved without many of the challenges feared. Grant professionals can play a key role as mentioned above, especially if the emphasis is removed from the grant opportunity and shifted to programs and services.

## ENDNOTES

(1) Taylor-Powell, Rossing, Geran "Evaluating Collaboratives: Reaching the Potential" University of Wisconsin Extension, 1998.

# Chapter 4 Checklist

## Organizational Readiness

| Indicator | Status |
|---|---|
| Do we have established relationships with other organizations within our field and in our geographical area? | |
| Do we collaborate with other nonprofits for service delivery? | |
| Are all our partnerships mission-centric or program-specific? | |
| Do our community partnerships enhance our credibility in the community and improve relationships with key constituents including funders? | |
| Have we explored administrative collaborations as a way to reduce costs or achieve economies of scale? | |
| Do we discuss potential partnerships with key funders before moving forward? | |
| Do we discuss new partnerships in a team environment involving staff from programs, marketing, and grants departments? | |
| Does each partnership have a collaboration plan, written documents of understanding, and a way to evaluate success? | |
| Do we and our partners make joint efforts in the areas of grant seeking, public relations, and program delivery? | |

## Grant Professional Readiness

| Indicator | Status |
|---|---|
| Am I aware of organizations in my community with partnership potential? | |
| Do I regularly inform my leadership about the importance of building partnerships and alert them to potential collaborators? | |
| Am I aware of funding opportunities that may be available to my organization for the purpose of collaborative efforts? | |
| Am I involved in partnership discussions between my organization and potential partners? | |
| Do I fully understand the joint benefits of our partnerships and am I able to communicate these to funders? | |

# Part II

# Creating the Request

# Organize the Grants Function

> *"When I am reading a proposal, it's very easy to tell if it was written by an outsider, such as a consultant. Contract grant writers need to become involved with the organization before writing for them. Become an on-site witness to the programs, much like auditing a class. Otherwise the request reads as though the writer is detached."*
>
> Patricia Stilley, Executive Director
> Sterling-Turner Foundation

Once the groundwork has been laid, leadership is energized, and various departments are communicating frequently from the highest to the lowest level, a more cohesive and efficient grant seeking effort is on its way to being established. Whether a grant professional is new at a position or not, he or she can organize the grants office with some simple steps that will go a long way in lessening chaos each time a proposal is to be written. Even in the grant professional's own domain, results will improve tenfold if other organizational departments, staff, and leadership are brought in for advice, input, and support.

## Analyze the Current Set Up

Some organizations have a simple grants office, with one grant professional who may or may not be responsible for other fundraising duties as well. In many ways, this simplistic model has the advantage of a more cohesive grant seeking effort, because there is less need for communication among different fundraising staff and more awareness of donors and stewardship processes.

Larger organizations often have a more specialized grant function, ranging from one or more part-time or full-time grant professionals working mostly in isolation; many of the largest organizations have highly focused grant efforts that may nevertheless suffer from a complete lack of communication across departments. On the other hand, very small nonprofits and community organizations may utilize a volunteer or even the executive director as a grant writer. Although these are generalizations, one can accurately predict that many nonprofits do have similar grant seeking set ups.

Our research found that 71.8% of nonprofits utilize a grant writer. Of the respondents who do not use a grant professional, 40.9% were *small budget* organizations, which is to be expected. Startlingly, 25% have *very large budgets*, again pointing to the fact that grant seeking is many times not considered a real fundraising department and the burden of writing grants is often given to other staff or volunteers not truly capable of or trained for the purpose (see Figure 5.1).

Backing this claim is the fact that of all the organizations not employing grant professionals, a large number utilize other development staff and even program staff for their grant writing needs (see Figure 5.2).

The ideal time to organize a grants office or work space is when a new grant professional is hired; however, such organizing can easily be conducted on an ongoing basis or during a down-time such as summer vacation for school-related nonprofits. Although most organizations use some sort of database or filing system to gather grants data, it is important to gather information manually as well in order to fully grasp how the grants office is working. First and foremost is an assessment of currently outstanding grant proposals using a simple worksheet. The information in this worksheet can be collected using

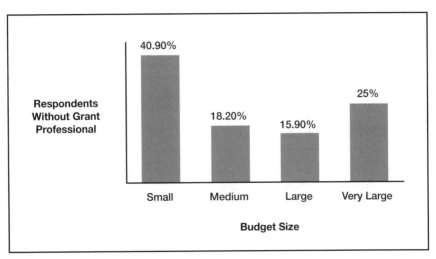

Figure 5.1 *Absence of Grant Professional by Budget Size*

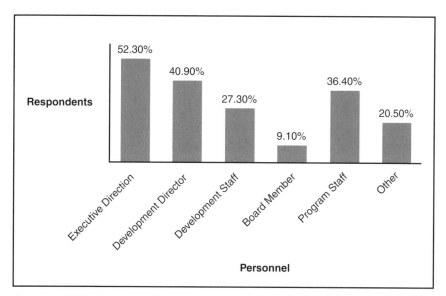

Figure 5.2 *Other Personnel Writing Grant Proposals*

the current database or filing cabinet, interviews with other staff members, and maybe even detective work (see Figure 5.3).

The purpose of this worksheet is simple: the grant professional gains an overview of outstanding grant proposals to foundations, corporations, and government entities that may either require follow-up or need to be discontinued. It also allows an in-depth understanding of how grant proposals have been submitted in the past and whether contacts at the organization (board members, volunteers, or program staff) have been utilized for possible connections or relationships. For grant consultants, this type of worksheet may be instrumental in keeping track of outstanding requests for multiple clients; however, care should be taken to include requests submitted by previous grant writers as well. This worksheet should be updated on a regular basis (quarterly or annually, for example) in order to assess the grants effort for pending requests from one worksheet to the next.

The grant professional should also regularly review lists of current supporters and use some type of trend analysis to compare how grant seeking

| Funder Name | Amount Requested | Purpose/ Project | Date Submitted | Expected Date of Award | Written By | Contact at our Agency |
|---|---|---|---|---|---|---|
|  |  |  |  |  |  |  |
|  |  |  |  |  |  |  |

Figure 5.3 *Pending Requests*

efforts are improving or declining. In either case, an understanding of the trends is essential to know how the grants effort is progressing and what challenges are being faced by the grants team. For example, a trend analysis of all applications to a certain foundation over the last five years may reveal that none have been funded, leading to a discussion of possible reasons, such as lack of board involvement as explained in Chapter 1 or absence of alignment with funder mission as explained in Chapter 6. Alternatively, a trend analysis may reveal that the amounts granted by a particular foundation have fluctuated over the years based on the type of request. Additionally, trends across requested projects or programs may reveal what type of requests or projects foundations are typically conducive to; for example, if multiple funders are observed as granting awards to an organization for capital expenditures but almost all proposals to fund a new project have been declined, it may be an indication that it is time for program staff and leadership to go back to the drawing board and analyze that particular program, its design, and evaluation. A discussion of possible causes of all these trends—both positive and negative—and brainstorming of possible solutions across departments is essential in order for an organization to move from a grant seeking to a grant strategizing approach which forms the basis of this book. Grant professionals can contribute significantly by discussing concerns with a few long term funders of the organization and bringing their feedback to the table; as Chapter 9 will show, many program officers at larger foundations are happy to provide their input about improvement areas in programs and projects.

Also, an incoming grant professional should conduct initial meetings with other fundraising staff, various program directors, and members of accounting and finance; these meetings should continue on at least an annual basis. The purpose of such conversations is to understand how each person or department is currently involved in the grants effort. For each person interviewed, as well as overall for each department, the grant professional should record the following information (see Figure 5.4):

| Name | Department | Involved Y/N? | Involvement (check all that apply):<br>• Prospect research<br>• Personal/professional relationship<br>• Received grant funds for programs<br>• Grant management function<br>• Stewardship function<br>• Grant writing<br>• Budget creation<br>• Other |
| --- | --- | --- | --- |
|  |  |  |  |

Figure 5.4 *Current Staff Involvement*

For each type of involvement listed, details should be recorded including specific grant applications as well as the interviewee's function, such as what aspect of grant writing he or she was involved in or which current methods of stewardship are being conducted. This information will result in a better understanding of current grant seeking practices and identify gaps in efficient practices. For instance, through these conversations it may be divulged that budgets for programs are being created by fundraising staff or that grant management involves accounting instead of program staff. They may also identify positive practices, such as good writers or personal relationships with funders that the grant professional may not have knowledge of. Additionally, if grants teams are not already assembled, these discussions may pave the way for identifying valuable team members and their roles based on strengths, weaknesses, and relationships. We will continue this topic later in the chapter.

Many grant writing experts recommend conducting interviews with program staff to learn about current and future programs. Although a valid approach that may be necessary for some grant professionals, this book advocates ongoing communication with program and other staff and regular involvement of grant professionals in all phases of development and implementation of not only programs but also marketing, public relations, and board development. If Chapters 1–4 are followed in letter and spirit, the grant professional will become an expert in many of those areas and will have no need to meet with program staff to learn about programs or projects. Of course, in some cases the interviewing may become necessary, such as for incoming grant professionals who were not present during the development and design of programs.

The final aspect of current set-up analysis is to collect and categorize important documents, making electronic copies if possible. These documents may be divided into three groups:

- Organizational documents: 501 (c) 3 letters, articles of incorporation, board of directors list, organizational chart, annual reports, Form 990, audited financials, key supporters, etc.

- Program documents: fact sheets, brochures, logic models, program diagrams and depictions as mentioned in Chapter 3, staff bios, resumes, partners lists, and current Memorandum of Understanding, client testimonials, etc.

- Proposal documents: master proposals and boiler plates, needs assessments or statistical data, position papers or research reports, etc.

Many grant professionals working at large and small nonprofits typically experience "stressful deadline syndrome" when a proposal is due but various attachments or appendices cannot seem to be found. The above collection of documents in a file cabinet or in the computer can save countless wasted hours and can reduce stress. Consultants may even request some or all of this paperwork to be on file before accepting a project, since these types of documents also serve to offer evidence that the organization in question has an orderly and professional working environment and is not a novice in grant seeking. The documents should continue to be examined every six months (more frequently for some program information) in order to ensure that the most current information is on file.

# Strategic Fundraising

One aspect of organizing the grants office has nothing to do with grant writing and everything to do with other development functions. The strategic planning process explained in Chapter 2 is just one area where a nonprofit can align mission and goals with specific organizational practices such as marketing or programs. Strategic planning at the micro-level also occurs in many organizations in fundraising, whether as part of the overall strategic plan or separately. It goes without saying that fundraising plans should be created with input from board members, senior leaders, and development staff; however, many resources for creating such plans are available for nonprofit organizations (1).

But while fundraising plans are quite common, adequate attention is often not paid towards the alignment of various development areas for a unified endeavor. If the fundraising plan has a fragmented stance, with each development area working more or less independently, the results promise to be less than spectacular because it will encourage an independent mindset among development staff. However, as part of the strategic development process, other fundraising staff, such as major gifts, special events, or planned giving can be motivated to improve communications and cooperation and build a more cohesive, smoothly-run development department that ultimately leads to grant seeking success. A good fundraising plan details not only the fundraising goals of each development area, but is a result of strategic planning within each development department as well as a combination of strategies across departments. For instance, instead of creating separate action plans and budgets for each development area, a strategic fundraising plan would determine how major gift officers would interact with special event staff or how the strengths of the capital campaign volunteer committee would be utilized for the benefit of the grant writing team. Similarly, at many large universities, the traditional responsibility of the prospect research unit is to support the efforts of the major gift officers, while the grants team researches its own funding sources. The premise of this book is that by working together in nontraditional ways, the entire fundraising staff will be able to generate more revenue and grant awards will also increase as a result. For instance, prospect research—discussed at length in Chapter 6—is just one area of fundraising that may work effectively with grant professionals to improve funding streams.

Small steps can be taken by the grant professional as well as the entire development staff to build unity and cooperation; fundraising calendars are one simple way to align efforts across development areas. Typically each area has its own calendar: event calendars tend to remain separate from capital campaign calendars and grants tracking in order to reduce confusion among staff and volunteers. A master calendar in different colors based on the different departments can be helpful in orchestrating activities as well as in reducing duplication; by including the deadlines, events and activities of program, and marketing and finance departments, the overall effort can be further enhanced. For instance, United Way agencies are restricted from individual fundraising during a black-out period encompassing several months when the United Way conducts its own solicitation; however, grant proposals may still be submitted to foundations during this time. A master calendar can make the entire development staff aware of these restrictions and act accordingly. Similarly, if program events such as a back-to-school fair or the opening of a new exhibit at a museum are included in the master calendar, major gifts officers and even grant professionals may be able to invite current or prospective donors or volunteers to witness the work of the organization first-hand. Some might argue that these types of notifications can be given to staff on a periodic basis throughout the year through other channels such as email or staff meeting announcements; the fact remains that many opportunities may be left on the table because of a lack of time for planning and execution. If the grant professional is on a deadline to submit a report or proposal, he or she may not be able to take suitable action unless the master calendar shows the upcoming event several months in advance.

One way to increase communication is by sharing documents, templates, and statements across development areas as well as within the entire organization, as long as consistency is maintained. This messaging may be as simple as using the same font or stationery in grant proposals as is used in marketing materials or creating a capital campaign case statement using language, pictures, and stories similar to those developed by the grants team.

Another technique to ensure that everyone within the fundraising department stays on the same page is by recording foundation prospects and current funders in the same fundraising database used by the rest of the organization. Too many nonprofits store grants data in spreadsheets or other less sophisticated programs because they either do not have access to what the rest of the development staff is using, or because the grant professional feels that the other databases are less oriented towards grant funders and more towards individuals. This suggestion does not imply that every organization should purchase an expensive fundraising database regardless of their financial situation or fundraising needs. Rather, whatever method is currently being used to store donor data should be used to store foundation data as well. If possible, copies of the actual grant proposals should also be stored in the same place, because it may be important to refer back to them periodically to see what was promised to funders.

---

### Best Practice: Rollins College

Rollins College in Winter Park, FL, utilizes separate fundraising departments, such as major gifts, alumni, foundations, and grants and contracts, working in collaboration with each other. The directors of each department meet twice a month to strategize and discuss the issues that might need collaboration. During these meetings, they divide prospect lists and determine which department will approach each prospect. If more than one department has the potential to receive a gift from a prospect, they discuss the best strategy to approach him or her; the grant professional at the college is consulted to find out whether that person might be associated with a foundation or if a foundation relationship already exists. The research department also plays a key role in this strategizing. A member of the Advancement Research department takes notes during these meetings and inputs into the database, assigning staff on the next steps of prospect management. He or she emails task sheets to everyone so that tasks and responsibilities are clarified and no mistakes are made. Once a task is completed, the appropriate staff member creates a contact report and inputs into the database. Once a month, the research department collects all contact reports and compiles a summary on what happened and whether tasks were fulfilled. The advantages to this collaborative system are numerous. It cuts down considerably, if not entirely eliminates, multiple requests to the same prospect, be it an individual or a foundation. It also results in more effective requests because it matches what is being requested to what a donor's interests are as discovered by each department. Through the collaborative model, the college can send out the best possible request. Even if other departments write and submit the actual request, this model ensures that the grant professional remains involved at all times and that his or her store of knowledge is best utilized for effective grant writing.

# Collaborative Grant Seeking

Collaboration outside of the development department is equally important to improve the grant seeking effort, first and foremost by ensuring organizational capacity and grant readiness. Concerns may range from "can we realistically serve 50% more clients based on current personnel levels?" to "what types of technology and infrastructure should we have in place in order to measure outcomes as required by this funder?" Grant readiness can be assessed through discussions with a variety of individuals on the following topics:

- What are the foundation's program requirements, and will our staff have the time and capability to fulfill them? This includes service delivery, external collaborations, volunteer capacity, staff expertise, and outcome measurement.
- What are the organizational requirements such as matching funds, equipment and facilities, or leadership involvement? What part will other departments such as public relations and accounting have to play?
- What is the financial cost of this grant versus the opportunity cost of not applying? This includes hiring additional staff, investing in technology, and costs associated with grants management. On the other hand, can some or all of the related costs be included in the budget?
- Are there any potential conflicts of interest or clashes with stated organizational policies? This includes ethical issues, financial involvement of board members, or nepotism. It also takes into account the overall goals, values, and philosophies of the organization.

For this reason, program leaders should participate in the decision to apply for specific grant opportunities; many times, grant professionals are excited about responding to a Request for Proposals, but program staff is hesitant either because of the reporting requirements or simply due to a lack of time to gather all the relevant data. Periodic meetings to discuss upcoming grant opportunities allows for collaborative decisions that everyone is committed to, especially the people who will be responsible for spending the grant funds. Such meetings also reveal valuable connections from the program perspective: potential community partners, existence of best practices, and past challenges that the organization should be aware of when moving forward with a proposal or after a grant has been awarded. Accounting, finance, and administrative staff can participate in the process by discussing matters such as budgeting restrictions, logistics, and the like.

In other cases, the responsibility to assess grant readiness or decide whether a grant opportunity should be availed rests with the grant professional. At large institutions, especially colleges and universities, a more formal process for the approval of a proposal concept is often used in order to curb unrealistic enthusiasm on the part of program staff, faculty, or others requesting funds. The Eastern Oregon University's Office of Grants and Sponsored Programs requires potential grant seeking staff and faculty to complete an online form called "Grant Identification of Institutional Issues" to ensure that all external requests align with the university's mission and goals and that proposals do not promise what they cannot deliver. The form consists of 10 questions that prospective applicants must answer, such as "do the proposed grant-funded activities require use of additional equipment or greater use of existing equipment that will require greater maintenance?" and "do the proposed grant-funded activities directly or indirectly put demands on our information technology infrastructure, and can we accommodate it?"

Additionally, external opinions and viewpoints can be valuable when organizing the grants effort and preparing for grant writing. Volunteers can be very useful participants in a grants team by providing information about possible funding sources and opening doors of foundations or corporations that typically do not accept unsolicited proposals. Some organizations may have access to peer advisors who may facilitate and guide the grant writing process, such as the "ArtsPeers Advisory Network" created by ArtsWisconsin. This network provides experienced professionals to arts organizations looking for outside perspectives and timely information in a variety of areas including grant writing. In organizations that do not have access to such professionals on a formal level, grant professionals can pave the way for informal advisory networks by building relationships with their counterparts at other agencies or by contacting local or regional grant maker associations for recommendations. Some foundations encourage nonprofits to seek advice from their staff during the proposal development process, while others offer specialized training on strategic planning and collaboration.

Going a step further, Community-Minded Enterprises in Spokane, WA, uses advisory committees for the application of grant proposals as well as during the implementation of grant projects. The committees consist of a group of community members and stakeholders charged with discussing possible funding opportunities, conceiving the grant project, and guiding the organization through challenges. If a grant proposal involves several agencies, the advisory committee consists of staff members of those partners as well.

The grant professional serves in many organizations as a coordinator of efforts across departments, rather than a grant writer in the strictest sense. For some organizations, a collaborative proposal writing method has shown success as long as consistency in language and messaging is not sacrificed; instead of a single writer crafting the proposal, each section is written by the staff person most intimately involved in that particular function or service. This concept is more common in larger organizations but less evident in smaller ones or those spread over different locations. However, care must be taken to ensure that the final proposal reads in a single voice, does not repeat information, or even use the same words multiple times; the task of this polishing ultimately lies with the grant professional.

---

## Best Practice: Henderson Mental Health Center

Due to organizational size and complexity of programs, the Henderson Mental Health Center in Fort Lauderdale, FL, utilizes a team approach to grant writing. A typical proposal involves not only program staff and Program Directors, but the Chief Operating Officer (COO) and finance staff as well; the Grants Coordinator (GC) manages the entire effort and ensures a polished proposal. After conducting appropriate research about the foundation and grant opportunity, the GC contacts the Program Directors and COO via email with a summary of all available information including fundable programs, typical grant award, deadlines, and any preconference workshops; they make a decision on whether to move forward based on the information provided. If these department heads are interested in applying, the GC sends them detailed information about the grant opportunity, and any proposal format or template provided by the foundation such as a list of questions or specific items to be covered in the proposal. If no template or list of questions is provided by the foundation, the GC creates one using its stated guidelines; this template highlights the areas to be addressed by each team member. When the narrative responses are received back from program staff and others, the GC reviews them to ensure that all the questions or items are appropriately addressed. The GC is responsible for determining how much of this information to include, as well as for translating technical jargon into laymen's terms. The team typically goes back and forth several times with revisions; the GC saves each version with a date so that no confusion arises. After the proposal is submitted, all earlier versions are deleted. Once the narrative is complete, the GC sends it to key people within the organization depending on their schedules in order to review and suggest improvements. The budget is created by the finance department and the program director, with input from the GC regarding issues such as allowable items; once complete, the budget is reviewed by the program director and the GC to check for discrepancies. By utilizing the collaborative writing model, the Henderson Mental Health Center places the decision to apply on program staff, reduces the amount of time a single person spends on each proposal, and ensures that multiple sets of eyes review the information being submitted. The end result is a higher quality proposal than the one written by the GC alone.

# Build Experience

Grant writing is a skill that, fortunately or unfortunately, is often gained through on-the-job training. Twenty years ago, even the possibility of grant writing or grants management courses being offered at universities and colleges was laughable, yet such classes and certificates abound today. Although in recent years the profession is gaining recognition in its own right—through the establishment of organization offering training and networking opportunities (for example the American Association of Grant Professionals) and credentialing examinations (Grant Professionals Certification Institute)—many grant writers do not have the knowledge, time, or understanding for sufficient skill improvement. Further, many nonprofits either cannot afford to hire full-time, professional staff or do not know what the correct mix of skills and experience of a grants professional should be before employing him or her. Our research revealed that more than half of all respondents used a highly experienced grant professional or team, while a close second possessed mid-level expertise. However, 14.2% of nonprofits surveyed used entry level grant professionals (see Figure 5.5).

It is always beneficial for nonprofits to invest in their grant professionals by encouraging ongoing skill development and networking. This may be done in the simplest form by paying tuition for related academic courses or meeting fees for attending monthly networking luncheons. It may also be done, if time permits, through in-house training by more experienced team members to not only grant professionals but also other department staff such as program staff and volunteers who may be part of the overall grant seeking process. Large organizations such as universities are especially invested in building the skill set of those writing grants due to the involvement of faculty

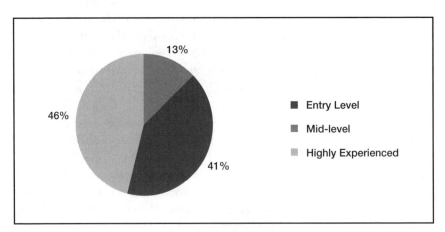

Figure 5.5 *Experience Level of Grant Professionals*

and staff in the grant writing process. Although the majority of nonprofits may never need such experience-building, some of the tools used by these colleges and universities may be adaptable to social service and even grassroots organizations.

Typically, only academic institutions, hospitals, and other big organizations possess the resources necessary to establish a department for supporting staff's proposal development efforts. However, grant professionals at smaller nonprofits, as well as consultants working for multiple clients, may send annual reports and email newsletters with regular updates and accomplishments to program staff and leadership. Informal trainings over lunch may

## Best Practice: Brazosport College

Located in Lake Jackson, TX, the Brazosport College's Grant Administration Office provides comprehensive grant support services to faculty, staff, and administrators as they seek and acquire grant funds. Recognizing that a thorough understanding of the grant seeking process will empower grant seekers and allow them to become active participants, the office not only prepares proposals in a team environment but also offers a variety of ongoing training related to proposal writing, logic model preparation, and collaborative relationship building. Going a step further, the office has established an internal competitive grant award called "Mini-Gator Grant," which allows college personnel to seek financial assistance for small projects while training them in the grant writing process. Applicants have to complete the proposal writing workshop offered by the office and abide by rules and restrictions, including reporting requirements, similar to those of outside funders. Although the grant awards are small, they are offered to 5 to 10 applicants on a quarterly basis, leading to motivation and skill development on the part of faculty and staff. Since the office is only a few years old, several other steps have also been taken to promote grant seeking on an institutional level and communicate progress. Twice a month, the office publishes an electronic newsletter posted to the shared network drive called "Grant News" with external grant opportunities, proposal development ideas, best practices in program development, education news and reports, and highlights of grants received by the college. The office also circulates a monthly flyer called "Opportunities Coming Your Way" matching specific grant opportunities to individual programs or departments within the college. Every year, an annual report announces the year's accomplishments and highlights, as well as a detailed grants activity report.

be implemented to train volunteers and staff members about those aspects of grant seeking in which the organization may historically be weak. In fact, these methods can form part of the overall effort to include all departments and areas including marketing, accounting, and fundraising in the process.

What constitutes expertise in a grant professional? Although this book does not favor any one training or certification over the other, the Grant Professionals Certification Institute examines certain competencies during its certification examination that are expected as industry practice from grant professionals (2). These competencies align with most of the major concepts imparted in this book:

- Researching funders and match requirements to programs (Chapter 6)
- Identifying organizational readiness for grant seeking (Chapters 1, 2, and 5)
- Involvement in program design and development (Chapters 3 and 4)
- Developing grant proposals and other funding applications (Chapter 7)
- Understanding grants management procedures (Chapter 9)
- Participating in professional development (Chapter 5)
- Creating and maintaining relationships with funders (Chapters 9 and 10)

In addition, this book suggests a much more intensive plan for the establishment of grant seeking strategies that include other areas of the organization and recommends a collaborative model that goes beyond the traditional understanding of the responsibilities of a grant professional. Grant consultants in particular often find that organizations seek their advice on other spheres of organizational development such as board development and program design, leading to the assumption that these areas have some contribution to overall grant seeking success.

The issue of expertise can also be considered from a program aspect, as explained to some extent in Chapter 3. For grant consultants in particular, as well as for new hires, it often takes time to understand the programs, service delivery model, and philosophy of the organizations they work for. Participating in program development meetings and becoming active participants in the design, development, and evaluation of programs can solve this obstacle by involving individuals in everyday operations and policy discussions. In fact, grant professionals should not be the only ones taking advantage of this proposition: volunteers and staff in marketing, accounting, and other fundraising areas—even board members—can also benefit hugely from this process. Participating in programs is another way to generate understanding and excitement: many Big Brothers Big Sisters agencies encourage their staff and board to become mentors, thereby ensuring that they are immersed in every aspect of the program from volunteer training to case management. Discussing the merits of the program with personal friends or in grant proposals then takes on an entirely new meaning and the quality of such contacts is improved tenfold.

Grant consultants in particular often face disconnect from the mission and programs of client organizations, especially if they are working off-site or have multiple clients in the same sector. These consultants should make it a habit to tour client facilities (meeting the people served, hearing their stories, and understanding the intricacies of the service delivery model) at the outset, as well as on a regular basis throughout the contract in order to stay abreast of program developments and witness the programs from a personal perspective. Most nonprofits will not suggest these visits unless prompted; hence, it is the responsibility of the consultant to include them as a part of the grant consulting process.

Columbia St. Mary's Foundation in Milwaukee, WI, grapples with a spread-out facility and hundreds of employees as it tries to streamline grant seeking efforts; it operates 4 campuses, a college of nursing, and more than 54 community clinics, and the foundation office is not located within the actual hospital facilities. As a result, there is danger of potential detachment between those working in the trenches and those writing the proposals and a possible lack of communication so essential to holistic grant seeking. To solve this dilemma and increase expertise in program subjects, foundation staff members are encouraged to participate in program planning; for example, when the hospital created centers of excellence to align itself in certain service areas, grant writers and other foundation staff members participated in the planning meetings to understand the process. They now continue to serve on a variety of leadership committees related to different service areas, thereby gaining specialized knowledge about those fields. In this regard, foundation staff uses a foundation-program-officer model of expertise, with each staff member having specialized knowledge about one or more clinical and health-related fields.

# Benchmarks and Evaluation

The question then becomes: how can the performance of a grant professional be judged? Various methods exist—some better than others—for assessing whether a prospective hire is a good fit for an organization, as well as to evaluate ongoing performance of grant professionals already working there. From the point of view of the grant professional as well, self-evaluation is an excellent tool to ensure that targets are met and superiors understand true indicators of success. The most common performance measure used by a multitude of nonprofits is the number of grants received or the success rate of an individual. However, discerning nonprofit leaders realize that in many cases, the skill of a grant professional alone is not sufficient to obtain funding, and that, as Chapter 6 explains, various factors apart from the proposal itself affect decisions made by foundation trustees in the boardroom.

It is for this reason that in stark contrast to other grant writing books, this one advocates a holistic approach to grant seeking and recognizes that board members and staff in marketing, programs, accounting, and even logistics can play a major role in the approval or rejection of grant applications. Therefore, it is usually unfair to judge the expertise of a grant professional based on his or her success rate. For grant consultants, this measure becomes even more confusing: different clients applying to the same foundation will tend to have different results depending on personal relationships, program design, public image, and much more. Usually, the grant office as a whole should be evaluated based on the following:

1. The number of proposals submitted during the year
2. The total amount of funds raised through grants
3. Ratio of proposals submitted to approved
4. Number of new foundations researched and approached
5. Number of first-time grants
6. Number of repeat grants
7. Stewardship activities such as number of reports submitted to current funders

Naturally, raw data on the above may not have any meaning unless the numbers are compared with those from previous years and some explanations of the reasons are tracked; for example, the number of proposals may decrease in a specific year because of a diversion of requests for a capital campaign, or the ratio of submitted to approved grants may rise due to a more aggressive submittal policy than in previous years. In addition, the grants effort should also track key "soft indicators" such as the number of board members who are involved in grant seeking and the number of funders with whom relationships have been built or improved.

An annual review of these items and a creation of upcoming benchmarks should involve not just grant professionals and their supervisors, but the entire grants team including program staff and senior leadership, thereby ensuring buy-in and commitment to the achievement of goals. Grant professionals should be evaluated based on their areas of responsibility and on the success of the overall grants effort instead of the total number or amount of grants received; for example, the percentage of time he or she spent on prospect research of new funders or the number of proposals worked on. Most importantly, creating and submitting a single grant request takes time and effort that should be judged qualitatively as well as quantitatively for maximum output.

## ENDNOTES

(1) See List of Suggested Resources.
(2) Competencies and Skills Tested, Grant Professionals Certification Institute. www.grantcredential.org/the-examination/competencies-and-skills-tested.aspx

# Chapter 5 Checklist

## Organizational Readiness

| Indicator | Status |
|---|---|
| Does our grants office have well-defined and easily-understood goals and objectives? | |
| Do we use trend analysis of grant efforts over the years to determine if program improvements are required? | |
| Do we have a grants team involving members from key programs and departments such as programs, public relations, and finance? | |
| Is our fundraising plan unified across development departments including grant seeking? | |
| Does all development staff work with each other to support and enhance all fundraising activities? | |
| Do we use the same fundraising databases for all development areas including grant seeking? | |
| Does grant seeking occur collaboratively within the organization? | |
| Does grant seeking occur collaboratively with other organizations? | |
| Are our grant professionals encouraged to build skills, expertise, and connections? | |
| Do we have an evaluation system for our grants department that takes into account a number of hard and soft indicators including board involvement and funder relationships? | |

# Grant Professional Readiness

| Indicator | Status |
|---|---|
| Do I have a good understanding of all currently outstanding grant proposals and their status? | |
| Do I use trend analysis to see if grant seeking efforts are improving or declining from year to year? | |
| Am I able to obtain feedback from funders about our grant seeking efforts? | |
| Have I conducted initial meetings with program staff and other employees of my organization to understand how they are involved in grant seeking activities? | |
| Do I have a method of collecting important boiler plate documents both in hard copy as well as electronically? | |
| Do I work with other development staff to create strategic fundraising strategies that include grant seeking? | |
| Do I work with staff from other departments to assess grant readiness and determine the feasibility of applying for specific grant opportunities? | |
| Do I regularly take action to improve my skills, expertise, and connections? | |
| Do I regularly visit our locations, meet with clients and volunteers, or otherwise keep in touch with the services being provided by my organization? | |

# Know Thy Funder

*"Before you even get to the proposal, my advice is to really know what you are applying for, and who you are applying to, and then to align your request with the mission of the foundation. You can have the best organization or the best program in the world but it won't get funded if you don't do the homework and the research before applying. Have some contact with the foundation beforehand, if that possibility exists. Don't send blanket proposals and most importantly customize your proposal to each foundation."*

Deena Epstein, Senior Program Officer
George Gund Foundation

G rant professionals know that research comes before writing, but many underestimate the time and effort it takes to identify funders who will be receptive to their request. However, it is rarely a waste of time to get to know who the proposal is being sent to, both on an institutional and a personal level. If the groundwork of relationship building has been set as discussed in this book's initial chapters, then half the work is already done. But if not, then the value of methodical and unrelenting research is even greater. Grant seeking is like sales: knowing who the potential customer is, finding out his likes and dislikes, and learning his communication style are all part of what makes a salesman a good closer.

## The Sea of Possibilities

Grant makers are as diverse as the people who work in them, and lumping all types together as foundations can be a mistake. Just as individual donors have their own needs and motivations for giving, so do institutional donors such as foundations; understanding what "makes them tick" is the key to successful grant seeking. Private foundations are a big part of the puzzle, and they are further divided into subtypes, depending on the reason they were created, the purpose they serve, and the people making their decisions. Within this group of funders, the most common types are independent foundations and corporate foundations; the majority of grant proposals that are written on a daily basis are submitted to these two major categories of funders.

A large number of independent foundations are further categorized into family foundations, where some or all of the decisions are made by family members. Families sometimes use this kind of foundation as a platform for family members to make charitable contributions in a formal manner and instill the value of charitable giving in future generations of the family. Family foundations are a mixed breed, from the informal to the professional. They range from those that are home-based and rely on holiday dinners to get together as a group and make funding decisions, to larger more structured groups with at least one staff member. Many small family foundations share professional staff and learn from each other when making funding decisions. Such foundations typically have generalized giving guidelines and more flexible application and decision-making processes. They also may give smaller grants and lean heavily towards nonprofits having relationships or affiliations with their trustees. In several cases, they do not accept unsolicited proposals, making the job of the grant professional much more difficult.

## Funder Perspective: The Siragusa Foundation
*Irene Phelps, President*

Q: How does the Siragusa Foundation operate and what factors help you make funding decisions?

A: The Siragusa Foundation is a small family foundation that has been supporting many of its grantees for a long time, some for more than 20 years. Because of that, we have developed strong relationships with those grantees and consider them equal partners. Even though we make the grant, they are the ones that are doing the work, which is our mission as well. Because our grants are small, we feel that our grantees shouldn't be spending hours completing our grant report. Of course, we want to know about their successes and failures, but not at their expense. Because of the economy, we have recently added nonmonetary support like educational sessions to already existing program and general operating support. One of the things that we are known for is our long term funding. However, we do fund new grantees once in a while; for example, one organization recently was recommended by my uncle who is no longer on the board.

The proposal was approved because his recommendation still has value. We also consider family history very important; for example, because my grandfather didn't go to college, we provide college scholarships; because he was a concert trained pianist, we support the arts.

Q: How do you recommend that nonprofits contact small family foundations, especially those that do not accept unsolicited proposals?

A: The first thing that a nonprofit should do is check to see if the foundation has a website and if so, review it thoroughly. Doing so can prevent wasted time and energy. If you have really done your research and feel that you are a fit for our priorities, send a brief letter of inquiry. However, even if you are a fit with our guidelines, if we are not taking unsolicited proposals, do not submit a letter of inquiry. Check the website regularly and call if you have questions. Family foundations are different from other types of foundations because of the involvement of family. In some cases, it helps to know a family member; in others, it does not. If you do know a family member, talk to him or her first to see if he or she would be willing to support your request to the foundation. Another way to connect with family foundations is for the nonprofit to ask existing funders to write a letter or call their colleagues.

Q: How do you find organizations worthy of supporting if proposals are generally not accepted?

A: We do our part in finding potential grantees based on the interests of the family. We go through the paper everyday to look at trends in our community, talk to other funders, and do research at the local regional association of grantmakers. Funders pay attention to what's going on in their communities and learn what the nonprofits are doing.

A considerable number of larger family foundations have transitioned into more formal structures with nonfamily members entering the board room and participating in decision-making. These foundations give out larger grants and create more structured guidelines, application procedures, and reporting requirements; other foundations that were founded many years ago may no longer have family members involved. However, the common bond between all family foundations is the set of values and goals they work by and which they inherited from their creator families. Most still give grants in the areas originally determined by the founding fathers and mothers of the family, and many remain loyal to the earliest alma maters, medical institutions, and other organizations that relationships were formed with. Interestingly, many corporate foundations share the same features, especially those that began from the vision of individual business owners and later grew to large corporate entities.

Some corporate foundations have formalized structures alongside family involvement, such as the Bill and Melinda Gates Foundation and the Dell Corporation, and therefore make grants based on the passions and interests of the families. However, the giving procedures of other corporate foundations are solely based on their corporate interests; for example, Motorola Foundation favors K-12 math and science education, while the Goldman Sachs Foundation prefers to support youth leadership, entrepreneurship, and business skills.

All private foundations are required to pay out at least 5% of their income per year to charitable causes, and this means that they have a purpose, just like the nonprofits they fund. In fact, foundations have missions very similar to those of nonprofits. They have visions of certain societal changes and goals of what their grants will achieve and are as determined as their nonprofit counterparts to accomplish their objectives by investing in their communities. As such, most foundations view the nonprofit sector as partners in the same cause. By recognizing this truth and appreciating the nuances behind it, grant professionals can identify which foundations to approach with the highest possibility of return.

Another type of funder that may be feasible to approach is the community foundation, which consists of donor-designated and donor-advised funds that have been created as alternatives to separate independent or family foundation. Although in many cases it is not possible to solicit funds directly from the donors making up the community foundation, some funds may from time to time issue Requests for Proposals. Community foundations also often have discretionary funds for which they conduct their own fundraising or several general funds from which to make grants to nonprofits. Such types of unrestricted gifts are very important to the changing needs and growth of the communities served by the foundations. The funds are distributed by the foundation to react to emerging needs, new programs, and ground-breaking services that might otherwise not get started or may not continue in the future.

Similarly, federated funds and federated campaigns such as the United Way sometimes offer unrestricted grants aside from affiliate support, which are based on a competitive grant application process. These funds range in terminology from "community building grants" (United Way of Greater Houston) to "community funds" (United Way of the Bay Area); they may even have a catchy name such as "Targeted Impact Fund" (United Way of New York City).

Because there can be so many different types of funders to choose from, each with their own purpose and giving strategy, it is important to decide which ones an organization plans to approach, and make a game plan about the when, how, and why before any contact is made. This may take days, weeks, or even months, depending on the amount of information available about the funder, and the number of people and departments within the organization involved in the grant seeking effort. Although generally it takes longer to conduct the research if more people are involved, at the same time the quality of data collected and the result of the effort is much higher if multiple areas of the organization are cooperating to seek grants.

# The Treasure Hunt

Once a target group of possible foundations has been identified using staff and volunteer relationships or through basic searches, the grant professional can begin to pare it down to a more realistic pool. Used mainly by larger institutions such as universities and hospitals, the field of prospect research is vast and can seem complicated to some. It also tends to focus more on individual donors than on foundations. However, by recognizing that intelligent and targeted research is a crucial factor in finding potential funders and building relationships with them, grant professionals at smaller or less savvy organizations can borrow the tools and techniques utilized by prospect researchers and implement them with modifications within their environments. Prospect researchers collect and analyze information about people and institutions (prospects) who have either given to an organization in the past or who may be motivated to give in the future. Although it is definitely easier to analyze a prospect after he or she has made at least one initial gift, it is also possible to use the same tools and techniques to bring prospective donors closer to making a gift or a grant.

The first step, as mentioned in Chapter 1, is to look for *connections* or relationships. These may be current relationships with staff members, volunteers, and even other organizations. Apart from direct relationships with board members or senior staff, it is also advisable to explore possible connections with other staff members and one-time volunteers. In some cases, even clients may become the source of building relationships, especially for academic institutions, hospitals, rehabilitation centers, sports organizations, and the like, which serve a large number of high-income individuals. Potential affiliations may exist outside the organization as well, for example community leaders, politicians, wealthy individuals, and supporters of similar nonprofits.

When searching for prospects within the world of family foundations, such relationships are even more important, because in many such cases, the foundation trustees make decisions based on their personal connections. Often, board members, staff, and other key players may not be aware of who they know in relation to who is being solicited. Rather than expect results in a vacuum, such as by circulating foundation trustee lists by email with the subject "do you recognize anyone?," grant professionals should learn to continually dig deeper and find nuggets of information such as colleges, churches, or business networking groups attended by the trustees. With a grant deadline looming, it is impossible to expect anyone but the largest organizations to do this kind of homework, but if done on an ongoing basis as part of prospect research, even organizations with one or two staff members can amass such details. When a board member looks at these "super lists" they may not see any names they recognize, but other information may ring a bell (see Figure 6.1).

| Trustee | Profession/ Area of Expertise | Corporate Affiliation | Religious Affiliation | Educational Background | Associations | Other |
|---|---|---|---|---|---|---|
| Mr. John Doe | Retired engineer | Vice President of External Affairs: ABC Engineering Company (retired)<br><br>Board of Directors: ABC Engineering Company (1990–1998) | Heavenly Heights Church | University of Houston: Bachelor in Science 1968 | Engineering Society of North America: member<br><br>Kiwanis North Houston: Secretary<br><br>Do Good Charities Houston: board member (2000–present) | Named "Good Samartian of the Year" by Kiwanis Club (2008)<br><br>Major donor for XYZ Hospital (2007)<br><br>Listed donor for following charities: ABC Health & Fitness $10,000+<br><br>Youth Help $5–10,000<br><br>Spouse Mary Doe, active in youth causes |

Figure 6.1 *Sample Super List*

Further, it can be more productive to schedule brainstorming meetings with staff, volunteers, or clients to come up with possible relationships to be further explored. For example Project Hope, an international health organization based in Millwood, VA, uses mapping exercises to identify relationships with foundations and other types of donors. Although mapping has many applications (organizations and governments throughout the world utilize it for asset and resource identification) grant professionals can conduct informal interactive sessions with small groups of people to map out potential relationships. The benefit of a mapping exercise is that the participants are open to new ideas and can brainstorm within a group of likeminded individuals. As a result, many previously unthought of affiliations may come to mind and be considered proactively.

Mapping can take the form of a list or a web as shown on the next page; more complicated mapping can also be conducted in the form of flow charts to show interconnections between multiple participants. Once these exercises are completed, the grant professional can use the results to determine which connections can be immediately accessed and which ones need more work. Then a strategy for prospect approach can be created with the help of the participants who suggested those particular connections (see Figure 6.2).

Within the group of funders identified through conversation, mapping, or other techniques, an attempt should then be made to learn as much as possible about their capacity for giving and their interest towards the cause. Both these types of information can be found using public sources as well as from the person with whom a connection has been made.

Prospect researchers use several resources to investigate the capacity or capability of a prospective donor to give. The signs of wealth may come from a variety of sources, such as the funders' websites, application guidelines, and other publications from the funder itself. Private foundations' Form 990-PFs provide detailed financial data such as assets, income, and investment activities, as well as actual grants awarded. Other signs of wealth may come from business news stories, society pages, and real estate publications related not only to the foundation but also its individual trustees. Especially in the case of smaller family foundations, this type of information may be crucial to determining capacity.

Additionally, prospect researchers look for the interest of the potential funder, which can be the most difficult to gauge. Often they have to dig deeper, look for clues, and explore the hidden past; one way to do this is to analyze the history and original mission of the foundation in order to understand donor intent. By knowing why and how a foundation was created, who the initial donors or founders were, and what they considered important, it may be possible to gauge whether the foundation is a good fit with the nonprofit's own mission and vision. An important note to remember is that many foundations across the country had humble beginnings, and its creators had true passion and interests in certain issues or causes that prompted them to create these grant making institutions.

Merely because a foundation on the target list grants funds within the organization's service area or has a similar mission (for instance, education or health), that does not automatically give the go-ahead to submit a grant application. One must be aware that information on funder websites or in guidelines is broad criteria, rather than specific conditions. When in doubt, it is always permissible to call the foundation and ask about its preferences;

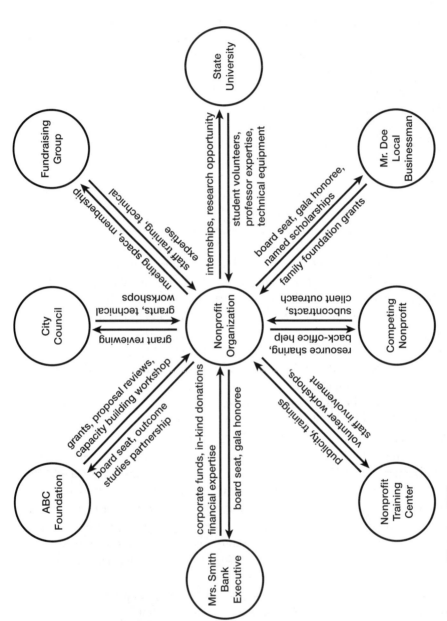

Figure 6.2 *Mapping Web*

there is no harm in mentioning the analysis of their grantee list or financials to say "I notice that although your guidelines say you fund operating expenses, your grants in the last three years have focused overwhelmingly on programs. If my organization needs general operating support, should we apply to you?"

Another way to discover what types of organizations a funder is interested in is to look at its previous giving history, although this may be easier said than done. As mentioned earlier, publications such as the Form 990-PF provides complete lists of grants awarded, which many smaller foundations do not publish elsewhere, and which can be great clues toward the foundation's interest. In this way, the grant professional can establish clearly the true geographic reach of the foundation (one specific metropolitan area instead of the entire state) and funding focus (all types of social services versus only one or two kinds). If a foundation funds all of New York State, but in the last two years all its grantees were located within the New York City area, then the chances of a rural organization receiving funds is slim. Or if a foundation claims to fund all educational endeavors but its giving history reveals that not a single grant was made to an institute of higher learning, a university should not consider itself a good fit. Some funder websites offer clues to what types of organizations, programs, or projects they prefer. The Robert Wood Johnson Foundation in New Jersey provides publicity to its grantees through extensive Grantee Profiles on its website, complete with grantee interviews, proposal synopsis, needs assessment, and sometimes even grantee videos. Further, many program officers and trustees participate in public events aimed at educating the grant seeking public, such as a panel discussion with area funders called Ink on the Page held annually by Grant Writers Network of Greater Houston and attended in large numbers by grant professionals from far and wide.

Therefore, by matching foundations' areas of interest and histories with the organization's own mission and programs, the grant professional can pare the target list to include only foundations that are a true match. However, the decision to apply or not rarely lies on the results of prospect research alone. As explained in Chapter 5, grant professionals who work with program staff from the very beginning of the grant seeking process can discuss the initial findings of the research with them and find out if, based on the criteria and requirements of the funder, it makes sense to apply. Reasons for rejecting a perfectly good match also exist: the reporting requirements may be too stringent for the organization to follow, or the deadlines to apply may be too soon for program staff or may lie in an unusually busy season. Similarly, by communicating with accounting staff, the grant professional may realize that a particular funder's maximum ask amount is too low to justify the work needed by accounting staff for initial recording and ongoing grant management purposes.

# The Human Connection

In addition to published guidelines, reports, and internet sources, the human element of prospect researching must also be appropriately recognized. As mentioned earlier, the origins and passions of a grant maker's founders can hold the key to understanding its current interests and giving priorities. Additionally, the current trustees and staff of targeted foundations may hold the key to funding priorities through their volunteerism and community roles. Many such people are vocal in their communities about issues they feel passionate about, and the foundations they are associated with may encourage this by seeking their recommendations and advice. Foundation trustees and donors often volunteer their time on nonprofit boards and attend special events of their favorite causes, thereby offering clues about their interest and inclinations. Although a more elaborate discussion on these human relationships and how nonprofits can benefit from them is offered in Chapter 10, it is sufficient for now to say that uncovering these types of community roles can be helpful in painting a clearer picture of some types of grant makers.

Just as family foundations may base their decisions on trustee priorities, corporate foundations often base their funding decisions on employee interests and community involvement. Recognizing that volunteers are a key source of not just expertise but also grants and corporate contributions, it becomes imperative to discover how companies in the area motivate their employees to volunteer and what methods of giving are utilized. A grant professional's research should therefore include the volunteer practices of local companies and businesses, the same way it includes foundation research. Some considerations are as follows:

- What constitutes the employee volunteer program? What are the program's goals and objectives? This will enable an understanding of whether the organization is eligible to participate and what approach to use, which is very similar to aligning foundation priorities to agency goals.

- Are employee councils used to make decisions? If so, which departments, positions, and actual employees are involved? This will help determine where and how to find corporate volunteers and what level of involvement may be attractive to the company. Such an analysis is similar to learning how foundations make funding decisions.

- How are nonprofits involved in the corporate volunteer programs? Are employee volunteer hours matched financially or are grants awarded to nominated organizations? Do events such as Days of Service offer opportunities to introduce nonprofits to employees? Answering these questions will help formulate a grant seeking plan of action that involves volunteers rather than directly approaching the company or foundation.

## Funder Perspective: Aflac Foundation
*Buffy Swinehart, Manager of Cause Marketing*
*Laura Kane, Second Vice President, External Communications*

Q: How does Aflac make decisions regarding funding, and what role do employees play?
A: The Donations Committee consisting of Aflac employees meets frequently during the year to look at proposals and make decisions. Typically, proposals recommended by customers and employees of Aflac have more weight; otherwise, they really need to be within our geographical area of Columbus, GA, or in our focus area of pediatric cancer. Relationships are key to our decisions; many times, we have given grants to other organizations that support the Aflac Cancer Center. We make an effort to find out who these organizations are and give them priority because of those relationships.
Q: How does Aflac motivate employees to become involved with nonprofits as volunteers and donors?
A: Although we always encouraged employees to volunteer, volunteerism has become very important to us in the last couple of years as we have learned what other companies are doing in the field. We track volunteer hours and in that way remain aware of the organizations our employees are involved with. We work with umbrella organizations such as United Way and Hands on the Valley and are able to advertise volunteer opportunities on our company intranet. We have also become more creative in our volunteer recognition efforts; we highlight a volunteer of the month based on number of volunteer hours, and during the year we name three volunteers of the year whose charities also receive donations. During our Volunteer Appreciation Week, we hold a volunteer fair to which organizations from the community are invited to participate.

# Ethical Considerations

Since prospect researchers collect and analyze a great deal of personal information about individuals and entities, such as salaries, wealth estimates, stock values, and biographical data, it is also imperative that they maintain a high level of ethics. The Association of Professional Researchers for Advancement (APRA) recommends that all those connected to prospect research abide by a code of ethics that includes issues such as privacy, confidentiality, and accuracy. Of special importance is APRA's Standard of Practices that offers guidelines for the collection, recording, and distribution of data. Regardless of whether an organization employs a professional researcher or conducts prospect research on an informal basis, these guidelines and code of ethics should be followed for an improved overall grant seeking effort.

Ethical considerations also include respect, especially of the stated and implied wishes of current and potential funders. It is neither respectful nor effective to send the same proposal to 20 foundations based on their overall giving focus or geographic location. At the least, it results in the proposal being thrown in the trash can, and at the worst, it can alienate the grant officer who is reading it. Although grant professionals are trained to follow instructions when writing the proposal, problems may arise when applying to foundations that do not have specific directions about what information to submit. Although some sections of a grant proposal are standard no matter who the funder, each foundation differs in what it finds important: one may be interested in program justification more than the other, while another may want an in-depth look at outcome measurements. Another foundation may want to know about a potential grantee's leadership and strategic goals, while another may consider the qualifications of front line staff more important. Taking individual trustee preferences and personal histories of family and corporate foundations into account, the going becomes even tougher. For these reasons, prospect research is truly valuable only when used in conjunction with conversation, strategic planning, and sometimes even the grant professional's intuition.

---

## Funder Perspective: Patrick and Aimee Butler Family Foundation
*Kerrie Blevins, Foundation Director*

Q: Can you explain the foundation's decision-making process and how proposals are judged?

A: Our decision making process is fairly transparent as far as processes and priorities are concerned. We are more likely to continue existing relationships than create new ones, although the latter does happen periodically. I conduct the reviews of proposals and make recommendations; some of which are intuitive based on knowing the board members' interests. As a program officer, I have to be familiar with the trends in the community that may have an impact on our giving. The process is very similar to a job application: what is written in the job description is only an outline or a guideline, and every applicant who fits the description will not get the job. There are a whole bunch of factors that may not be obvious to the nonprofit, such as payout, other commitments, etc. Just because we fund programs for teens doesn't mean we want to fund every program for teens that exists. We try to balance out across interests and community needs.

Q: What advice can you offer to nonprofits attempting to seek grants from foundations that accept proposals by a competitive process?

A: My advice to nonprofits is to learn about the foundation from its own materials rather than relying on outside resources such as the Foundation Center or the Minnesota Council of Foundations. Most of the time, those organizations do not have the most updated information. It's better to go to the primary source of information available, whether it is the funder's website, published reports, etc. All other sources should be secondary. Typically, too little time is spent on research by nonprofits. It would be more viable to spend energy on researching and finding foundations that are likely to support you and then contacting them to discuss your proposal. I think a lot of times the sense is that let's get the word out about our organization and maybe someone will fund us. In recent times, the transition to email can be difficult for funders because people are sending us Letters of Inquiry or even mini-proposals via email. The level of expectation is changing and nonprofits want more intensive relationships with funders. On the other hand, family foundations are least equipped to respond to that level of inquiry. The best approach is to submit a proposal if you fit the guidelines. Many nonprofits think of grants as a used car sale: send a proposal that falls outside the guidelines just to "shake it up" and get our attention. At the Butler Family Foundation, we conduct strategic planning every 3 to 5 years so we know what we should be focusing on and nonprofits should respect that. For a nonprofit that has never been funded by us, the proposal process and following all guidelines is critical to introducing the idea. It is also very apparent to us if a blanket proposal has been submitted. Although it's okay to send the same proposal to multiple foundations, the general "dear friend" approach never works. Usually such proposals don't explain the program in detail, don't request a specific amount, and don't use the application cover sheet.

Unless the grant professional knows what each foundation on the prospect list finds important based on its history, mission, and goals, the quality of proposals being submitted will be poor and the lack of research will be obvious. As already discussed in the previous chapter, organizations that have prospect research departments must work in tandem with grant professionals rather than as a separate unit supporting the major gifts or planned giving teams. For smaller nonprofits with little or no prospect research expertise, the grant professional is in the ideal situation to learn the basics of this field and improve the grant seeking effort using scientific methodologies and professional tools rather than the hit-or-miss approach.

# Chapter 6 Checklist

## Organizational Readiness

| Indicator | Status |
|---|---|
| Does the grants department have an overall plan for prospect research that may or may not include professional researchers? | |
| Do we encourage interdepartmental teamwork including the involvement of board members in order to research possible affiliations and relationships with funders? | |
| Do we place adequate emphasis on ethical prospect research? | |

## Grant Professional Readiness

| Indicator | Status |
|---|---|
| Do I have a good understanding of the various types of grant making entities? | |
| Do I have working knowledge of local funders' requirements and restrictions? | |
| Am I aware of all possible connections between my organization and potential funders, including personal and professional connections with staff, board members, clients and volunteers? | |
| Am I aware of the level of local funders' interest and capacity to give to my organization? | |
| Am I aware of the employee volunteer programs of the major companies in my area, and do I inform my leadership about potential grant opportunities through volunteers? | |

# Craft Winning Proposals

---

*"In any foundation, we look for a balance between the emotional pull and the data. We are generalists, not specialists, and we rely on nonprofits to explain the need and the programs."*

Kerrie Blevins, Foundation Director
The Patrick and Aimee Butler Family Foundation

---

Even though the term "grant professional" is relatively new to the fundraising field, people have been writing grant proposals almost as long as nonprofits have existed to seek funds and funders have existed to give them. Grant proposals have become more polished over the decades, and as the competition for grant funds is increasing—and the accountability of grant awards is gaining attention—the content of a typical grant proposal has become refined almost to the point of being an art. The number of people entering the grant writing profession is growing rapidly as the field comes of age through the establishment of organizations such as the American Association of Grant Professionals. At the same time, the number of books, trainings, and online resources teaching the basics of grant seeking is growing by leaps and bounds, implying that organizations and consultants are realizing the need for advanced skills in grant writing and management. Rather than repeating the step-by-step grant writing information so readily available elsewhere, this chapter focuses on strengthening key aspects of a proposal and addressing specific needs, situations, and circumstances.

# Typical Versus Extraordinary

Many foundations have guidelines regarding the content, format, and order of proposal narratives; several funders, especially corporate foundations, now have online applications which take the uncertainty and creativity out of grant writing. However, the majority of funders have few specific rules about what to include in a proposal or the extent of details necessary. When applying to such foundations, the typical proposal should be five to seven pages in length and include as many details as possible without seeming pedantic or complicated. The order of the sections or topics within the proposal can vary depending on the type of proposal; operating support proposals may include the justification section first and the organizational background later, while capital or project requests may discuss the need in subsequent pages once the goals and accomplishments of the organization have been clearly established.

Many grant professionals prefer to create a master proposal or template first; an all-inclusive document to be later used for smaller proposals and to answer specific funder questions. This method is not only beneficial for looming deadlines, but also enables program staff to become more involved in the grant writing process. Rather than writing in a vacuum, the grant professional can seek details from program staff and other department heads in order to write a more comprehensive version of the typical proposal, which can then be pared down as needed for specific funders (see Chapter 5 for a discussion on team grant writing). Also, senior staff and volunteer leaders can be asked to tackle in advance the strategic issues that will need to be addressed in every proposal: sustainability, community involvement, mission alignment, and the like.

# Proposal Content and Format

Although there are no rules about format or content other than those specified in funder guidelines, grant professionals can improve the quality of their proposals and polish their writing styles based on some basic rules of thumb:

*Executive Summary and Request Statement (half a page)*: Although not required in many foundation guidelines or literature, both can go a long way in clarifying the gist of the proposal upfront and saving the time of the program officer. The executive summary should include salient data from the needs assessment, as well as key information from the program description and evaluation sections. The request statement, similarly, should be

## Funder Perspective: Dwight Stuart Youth Foundation
*Wendy Chang, Program Director*

Q: What determines the overall quality of a proposal?

A: A lot of times, nonprofits forget that it is people who are reading their proposals. The stories are important and then data and statistics should be weaved in sparingly. In order to make an impression, it is incumbent upon them to create an emotional connection. Make sure that the funder can identify itself and see how it has a role in the story. Explain to us how we can benefit you. The most frustrating thing to me is the inability of nonprofits to be succinct. . .after all I have to sell it to the board. Just like any good marketing campaign where the product is change, one talks about the solution. It is difficult for us when a nonprofit continues to talk about the problem and uses extensive statistics to show the need. We are making grants because we believe that the problem exists and that some systems can bring about change. So don't just talk about the problem but tell us about your approach to change. . .your solution to the problem.

Another thing I have found is that people rarely spend time on a good case statement. Organizations spend two days on strategic planning that sits on a shelf, but not on the practical aspects of their organization. If people spent two days honing down a good case statement, they would be better off. Investing the time and resources up front on the case statement will be extremely valuable in the long run. Instead of hiring someone to conduct strategic planning (although that is also important) bring your stakeholders together and pound out a case statement because it needs to be something people, including funders, buy into. In reality, it is a marketing package that sells your message, and your proposals will be better off because of it.

very clear in stating the amount of the request, as well as any other relevant information such as the lead gift funder and the purpose for which funds will be utilized. As an example: "We invite the ABC Foundation to join our other donors, including the XYZ Foundation, through a grant in the amount of $50,000. Your support will go toward program costs and technology needs of our literacy campaign."

*Justification of Need (one page)*: Many organizations tend to gloss over this section, especially if the need is obvious. However, explaining the need from the community's perspective as well as aligning it with the mission and goals of specific funders can make the difference between acceptance and rejection of a grant proposal. Every grant professional explains the need in a different style and uses varying types of information. However, the key to writing a good justification is to use a mixture of emotional and analytical styles and to bring to life the need not only on a national or state level, but of specific local communities and clients as well. While writing this section the grant professional should take the following into consideration:

- What is the current situation of the organization's cause (a) nationally, (b) regionally or on a state level, (c) or locally in the communities being served? This should include not only statistics but also the human interest angle—for example, when describing the rates of breast cancer, describe not just the latest data but also the fact that it leads to children losing mothers and husbands losing wives. When talking about homelessness, include a description of faces and voices, not just numbers. It is perfectly acceptable to exercise the emotional touch as long as it does not go overboard.

- What is the ideal situation that the entire field in general and your organization in particular is striving to achieve? This answer should encompass the issue on a broader scale than just the one specific issue. For instance, when discussing theatre or art programs for children, mention studies proving the effect of such programs individually (on academic performance, social development, and even cultural and racial tolerance) as well as economically (such as on tourism and tax revenues). The focus areas and goals of the foundation being approached should be kept in mind when writing this part of the justification; in some cases, a foundation's guidelines may shed light on a specific angle that they may be more interested in funding. In that case, the justification could spotlight the one issue in detail rather than several issues. For example, lower graduation rates of at-risk students can lead to a myriad of problems ranging from the basic (juvenile crime or lack of future economic and educational opportunities) to the more complex (long term poverty, homelessness, health issues, incarceration rates, and much more). An organization applying to a funder whose stated interest is crime or homelessness should focus this section more fully on that aspect of the "ideal situation" rather than the entire gamut of indicators.

- What are the causes of the gap between the current and desired situations? This is the part of the justification that should impress the proposal reviewer through an in-depth and sympathetic analysis of local or regional issues. For a health organization, the causes could be identified as a lack of education or support to certain at-risk populations, whereas a vocational or trade school could explain the lack of resources available to area schools and universities to meet educational challenges. Again, a mixture of data and nonstatistical information should be utilized to best explain the causes in a compassionate manner, quoting from studies and reports as well as from more qualitative sources.

- What can be done to fill the gap? This is the bridge between the justification section and the subsequent description of programs or projects (see next item below). In a few sentences, the grant professional should explain what the organization offers as an answer to the problem described above; if there is a lack of leadership programs for girls, the answer may lie in comprehensive gender-specific mentoring programs offered by a specific organization. However, this statement or description should be generic rather than program or service specific: for instance, "seniors who regularly attend social events with their peers report lower incidents of depression and suicide; our organization recognizes that the senior population requires attention and involvement in order to fully flourish and remain physically and mentally healthy."

*Organizational Background (one to two pages, may be longer for operating support proposals)*: This section should follow naturally from the previous one, almost as if picking up the discussion where it left off earlier. Whereas the justification describes the overall need, the background explains how the applicant organization is best suited to meet it. As mentioned above, the sequence of sections will differ based on the type of proposal; therefore, when writing a proposal for a specific program or project, the organizational background may come before the justification section, which may then be followed by the program description.

Regardless of size, scope, and familiarity with the funder, the organizational background is essential to the grant proposal. In addition to the organization's history, mission, and accomplishments, care should be taken to explain what makes the services and programs stand apart from other similar organizations. Under the heading of "Competitive Advantage" or "What Makes Us Unique," this subsection could include a brief discussion on better outcomes, highly trained volunteers, state of the art equipment, regional partners, backing from a national organization, or being the "first" or "only" organization in any capacity. It is acceptable to name competing agencies when describing how their programs compare; however, it is important to ensure that accurate information is provided during this comparison and no negative comments are made about competitors.

Bering Omega Community Services in Houston, TX, uses comparative cost measures to create a truer picture of the impact of their services by explaining that "a day of inpatient care at our residential hospice costs $240 to provide services, compared to a day at a semi-private hospital $600." Their proposals explain how their services can save taxpayers millions of dollars by being an affordable alternative to the public health care system.

*Program Description (two or more pages)*: This is the meat of the grant proposal, and should explain the program or project's goals and objectives, methodology and service delivery, plan of operation/implementation or action plan, clients served, and collaborations. In requests for general operating support or overall program support, it may be advisable to break up the narrative into subsections addressing each major program offered. The subsections can then include a brief description, goals and objectives, and other relevant information for each separate program. This strategy is useful when an organization's programs or services are distinct or varied; for example, a musical group offering a wide range of programs for a variety of audiences, or a health center providing a mix of services to distinct sets of clients.

Alternatively, the grant professional can create a proposal for an "umbrella program" that encompasses a collection of related initiatives, programs, or services under a specific name such as "Community Based Services for At-Risk Youth" or "Serving More Seniors." While this name may only be on paper, it allows the grant professional to describe operating or program needs in a comprehensive way by combining client data, outcomes, overall goals and objectives, and budgetary needs. It also gives more flexibility to grant managers when using and allocating grant funds.

Often grant professionals leave out some key elements of a program description unless specifically required: specifically, key staff qualifications and implementation timeline. Although a timeline may not be useful for ongoing operating support, having some kind of timeline for program activities can be extremely helpful to the proposal reviewer. Similarly, the qualifications of key program staff, whether directors or field staff, can present a powerful argument for the potential success of the program, and hence should be included as long as the qualifications or experience of the staff members are at par with requirements. For example, in operating proposals, the experience of the executive director and other senior staff in both administrative and fundraising functions can be very valuable, whereas in program proposals the highly technical degrees of front line staff not only prove expertise but also offer a competitive advantage over other organizations. Chapter 2 provides a sample staff bio-data worksheet which can be utilized for collecting and updating this type of information on a regular basis.

*Outcome Measurement (half a page)*: Many grant professionals include outcomes in the program description, while others do not mention them at all unless specified by funder guidelines. However, the reality is that whether required or not, outcome measurement is often the key to getting funded, and grants are often awarded based on expected results and overall success factors. Evaluation has become almost a buzzword in grant maker circles,

## Funder Perspective: George Gund Foundation
*Deena Epstein, Senior Program Officer*

Q: How can applicants show creativity and stand out among the thousands of proposals seen by a program officer?

A: Clear and to-the-point writing is very important. My background is journalism, so I like to see the "who, what, why, when, and how" right off the bat. Tell us right at the beginning what you are looking for; don't spend pages and pages trying to come to the point.

Q: What types of information can be included in the proposal to establish the need?

A: It all depends on the foundation being applied to. If you are applying to a foundation that has very broad criteria or if they fund a very large geographical area, you may have to use data and statistics to back up your request and explain the need in your area. But many foundations have very specific areas of interest and so chances are that they already know those issues very well. So in those cases you don't need to include lots and lots of data and statistics trying to convince them that the need exists: they already know that the need exists. It is more important for the organization to explain why it is the one to address that problem, whether because of staffing, history, programming—whatever makes it more qualified to address the issue. Spend more time building the case for your organization, rather than drowning the program officer in data. If you are limited by the amount of pages you can submit, give a teaser in the proposal and add more details such as staff bios, statistics, etc., as appendices.

Q: What do you look for in the program or organizational description?

A: We look at the organization's track record; for example, has it ever done this kind of thing before or does it have the capacity and the staffing to do what they are promising. We look for a strong and engaged board and financial stability as well. Thirdly, we look at whether the organization is woven into the fabric of the community—what's the relationship with the community they are trying to serve, do they have local people involved in the staff, the board, or through collaborations? The program methodology isn't as important as some of those things.

but it is a process whose importance is bound to grow rather than fade away with time, as issues of accountability and sustainability come to the forefront. Chapter 3 contains a detailed account of how to create an evaluation process within an organization or a specific program; several external resources can also be used to develop a comprehensive outcome measurement plan (1).

The evaluation section of the grant proposal should discuss the expected results of the program or project by explaining succinctly what it hopes to achieve, such as improved academic performance, reduced crime rates, or improved health conditions. The more detailed and program-specific the expected results, the higher the likelihood of the proposal reviewer understanding the key issues as they relate to the organization's goals and objectives. Also, the narrative should distinguish between short-term outputs (for example number of students mentored), medium-term outcomes (such as improved self-esteem), and long-term community impact (for instance, lower drop out rates). Another important aspect of outcome measurement is the methods and sources to be used: the main evaluation tools and resources such as feedback forms, surveys, pre- and post-tests; the timeline for overall as well as intermediate data collection, and the persons responsible, including any outside evaluators.

Funders are increasingly recommending and even requiring logic models to depict the entire program in general and the evaluation process in particular. Several resources are available for grant professionals who wish to learn about this popular tool (1). However, it is important to seek guidance from program staff, especially those involved in outcome measurement, before developing a logic model.

*Sustainability (half a page)*: As the competition for grant dollars becomes fiercer and the number of smaller nonprofits increases, funders are becoming more interested in long-term sustainability than in immediate results. Many organizations with innovative programs are finding that, instead of dazzling funders with their novelty, they have to prove continuity and persistence in a variety of ways. Although relatively few funders currently ask applicants to discuss how the program or organization will be continued after the grant period, grant professionals are expected to thoroughly address this vital issue in every grant proposal, in conversation with program officers, and in site visits. How this question will be answered depends on the input of not only program staff but also senior officials, board members, other donors, and even collaborating agencies. The justification for sustainable programs should be built upon one or more of the following:

1. Current fundraising model: what are the main sources of income for the organization as a whole? Funders like to see a diversified funding stream rather than reliance on grants; they also want to know how many individual funders, including board members, are financially supporting the organization's efforts. The best way to showcase a funding stream is to give percentages of income from the major sources such as special events, individual donations, government and foundation grants, and the like. A brief discussion of any

new fundraising or marketing initiatives is also advisable if they prove an effort by the organization to increase or diversify funding from a variety of sources.

2. Future support: are there any long-term grants, donor pledges, or other major sources of support such as endowment funds that can be utilized in subsequent years? This could be in the shape of unrestricted monies for the entire organization or specific funds earmarked for the requested program or project. Not only does this prove the ability of the organization to carry on after the grant is used, but also establishes peer approval in the eyes of the funder.

3. Earned income: does the organization have the potential to generate revenue and if so, is there a business plan for appropriate implementation? Some organizations charge clients a nominal fee for the provision of goods or services, but the majority is entirely supported by grants and donations. However, funders are now becoming aware of the shortcomings of this "humanitarian" model, as it leads to reliance on outside help and a lack of motivation in becoming self-sufficient. Organizations should explore mission-centric ways to generate revenue: thrift sales, sliding scale fees, corporate sponsorships or cobranding agreements, and vehicle donation programs, to name a few.

4. Internal contribution: what does the organization itself bring to the table? The proposal should explain the in-kind and volunteer contributions of the organization as a whole, as well as for the requested program or project. In addition, any infrastructural and technological value already built in (such as a rent-free building or a newly installed database system) is also an advantage from a funder's viewpoint because it not only results in reduced costs but allows for sharing of resources across programs and services.

5. Organizational stability: how long has the organization been in existence and how well-established is it in the community and among its stakeholders? By discussing brand recognition, collaborator confidence, and even outcomes, the proposal can attest to the long-term stability of the organization and its ability to attract funds in the future. Any current plans for marketing, program improvement, and other significant changes should also be highlighted.

6. Strength of leadership: is the board of directors financially committed to the organization, and what steps are taken to ensure 100% board giving? Again, this points to long-term stability and community connections.

## Funder Perspective: Philadelphia Foundation
### R. Andrew Swinney, President

Q: How can nonprofit organizations prove sustainability and investment-worthiness?

A: Any organization regardless of size has to explain the following three things in their proposal; for small nonprofits, these explanations become even more critical. The first issue is whether they are broadening their base of support. For the most part, this means individual support, but it is important to explain the multiple streams of revenue that are available to them. The second question is: do they have a plan? They should be able to clearly show how they are going to proceed in the next three years; not a strategic plan, but a management plan. One example of how such a plan could be explained is through budget projections. It suggests to a funder that this nonprofit is seeing beyond its nose, planning for success and the future. They should have a road map of what their business plan is to be successful, and how they will get there. Are they thinking seriously about operating expenses that they will face two or three years down the road? Do they know what it will cost to achieve their goals, and how they will raise the money needed to match those expenses? Have they thought about what kind of financial and programmatic issues they will face in the future? Thirdly, what do they need help for? Based on their projections, nonprofits should understand which area they need the most help in. The three main areas are revenue generation (i.e., funding), administration (i.e., financial management), and program delivery. If they ask for operating expenses, it may mean that they have not really created a plan as I have explained previously.

Q: How do you assess requests for programs compared to requests for operating support?

A: When we see requests for general support, we tend to ask whether the applicant has even considered how they will get the general operating support in order to get where they are going. Have they looked at their three-year plan and explained how they will handle financial management practices, the need for technology, for example? How will they increase program revenue and what kind of administrative practices will they take, for example, in marketing or public relations? If they are planning to increase donations, do they have an actual plan or a body of personnel who will solicit funds from the community? Organizations that ask for operating funds often have a mindset that this is what we do as an organization and hopefully funders will fund us. On the other hand, someone who comes to us and says, I am a businessman with a mission to deliver XYZ services, I have a three-year plan of what I want to achieve and how I want to grow, here's my budget, and what I need the most help in is "this" area, as a funder I will understand this approach much better and want to fund it.

The above discussion of proposal content and format allows the grant professional to judge whether one aspect of the narrative is overshadowing the others or if certain important areas are being insufficiently addressed. Also, as mentioned previously, operating requests may have a slightly different format than project requests. For example, the organizational background section may be much longer and more detailed than the program overview. Thirdly, certain organizations may need to include diagrams and other visual depictions in order to explain complex issues or models, thereby increasing the length of some sections of the narrative.

Organizations may also deviate from the above rule of thumb format due to other reasons, such as a very large number of programs or services. Since many foundations tend to look unfavorably at proposals that go beyond six to eight pages, it may be better in such a situation to include program details as an attachment rather than increase the length of the proposal unnecessarily. Therefore, for an organization that offers several 15 different after-school programs, the narrative may include only a brief overview while the program details (program names, client demographics, timings, staff, and collaborators) may be explained at length in the appendices.

*Appendices and Attachments*: Proposal attachments vary by organization as well as by funder requirements. Some foundations have a strict rule about not including any additional documents, while many online applications grant applications do not offer applicants a field for attaching documents. Aside from these types of limitations, appendices can be a valuable means of providing a clearer picture of an organization in several ways:

- Graphs or charts related to program justification or outcome evaluations—these may be agency-specific or for the discipline as a whole.

- Position papers or studies linked to new programs or experimental methodologies.

- Program overview or fact sheets in cases where the list of programs or projects is too lengthy or detailed, or if the narrative only addresses one program or project in particular. Our research found that 55.4% of respondents included program brochures in their proposal packets.

- Visual representations and artist renderings of capital projects.

- Vendor quotes, signed contracts, and external evaluation reports, especially for requests related to the purchase of equipment or products.

- Client pictures or stories that have a direct bearing on the proposal—as will be explained in the next chapter these should be used sparingly, and decisions must be made regarding their appropriate placement. According to our research, 26.1% of respondent nonprofits included client pictures with their grant proposals.

- Agency newsletters, press clippings, or other marketing material if directly related to the proposal—for example, if the narrative includes references to accomplishments, commendations, or awards received.

- Staff bio-data or qualifications—although best included within the proposal, some cases may require an attachment: for instance, if the number of personnel is more than three or four or if the list of qualifications is very long. Our research discovered that 45.2% of respondents typically attach senior staff bios to their narratives.

- List of collaborators—although best suited for the narrative itself, the list may be so long or the details of each collaborator so extensive that it would take up unnecessary space.

- Letters of support, MOUs, and other supporting documents—while of limited value to established organizations, these can be extremely helpful for newer organizations as they attempt to improve their credibility with funders. Our research found that almost 20% of respondents "always" include letters of support or recommendation in their proposal packets, while 6.4% "never" do so (see Figure 7.1).

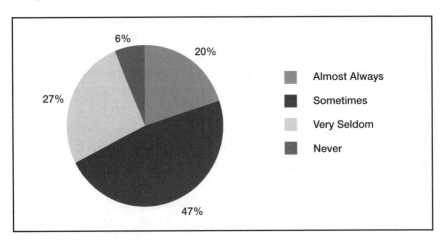

Figure 7.1 *Use of Letters of Support*

*Budget*: Although budgets should remain the primary responsibility of program and financial staff, many organizations place the burden of budget development on grant professionals due to lack of adequate staff or time. A better approach, as explained in Chapter 3, is designing and developing programs through team work; this ensures that all relevant parties are involved in the process to give expert advice about the use and distribution of grant funds. Operating support proposals typically only require overall operating budgets developed as part of the organization's annual planning and accounting; however, problems often occur when submitting proposals for specific programs, projects, or capital expenditures. Below are some common scenarios and how to deal with them.

- The proposal is for a small portion of the entire program budget, and the grant professional creates a budget specifically for one foundation's grant. This is a major blunder from the point of view of accountability and ethics; it is also likely to present confusion for program staff in the future by creating multiple budgets for the same program. Each program and project should have its own budget created annually or at the beginning of its life; the grant professional should include this budget in the grant proposal after ensuring that it is accurate, especially if there are changes in staff or expenses have increased recently.

- The proposal is for a new program that does not have a formal budget yet but its implementation has been accelerated due to a grant opportunity. Apart from the ethical issues and subsequent program difficulties that arise whenever a project is "created" in order to take advantage of an attractive grant opportunity, the grant professional remains in a quandary as well because of a lack of understanding of true program needs and expenses. The correct approach is to evaluate every project based on its merits and to develop a comprehensive budget based on actual costs using strategies explained in Chapter 3, or any other method regularly utilized by the organization. It is the grant professional's responsibility to inform program and finance staff about any funder restrictions or requirements pertaining to that specific grant opportunity.

- The organization does not possess any program-specific budgets. This is often the case with small organizations that operate with very few staff, and the person responsible for writing grant proposals is expected to create budgets whenever grant opportunities arise. As explained in the previous scenario, developing budgets based on grant opportunities is a risky approach for a variety of reasons. It is better to first attempt to reorganize and improve internal processes and develop budgets for programs, even if they are simplistic in nature. If an important grant opportunity arises in the meantime, the grant professional and staff or volunteer leaders should meet to develop a budget for the program in question, trying to stay as true to the real picture as possible.

- The organization has separate budgets for internal and external uses. Again, considerable ethical questions may surface as a result of this duality, and care must be taken to understand why separate budgets may be necessary. Some nonprofits prefer not to disclose the details of expense allocation to funders, while others show more details in the revenue sections in external budgets than they do in internal documents. As long as the budgets are the same in numerical value and reflect true income and expenses, it should not present a problem. However, if they are different, then the grant professional must take responsibility to discuss potential funder concerns with senior staff and to ensure that the most accurate information is being presented to all stakeholders.

- The foundation requires that its own budget template be submitted with the proposal. This is often the case with corporate foundations and those with a broad geographical scope; the purpose of the templates is to streamline the budgets of various applicants so that each category is comparable. The grant professional may find it easier to complete the template in isolation, as long as the categories are more or less similar to the actual program budget. However, many templates require input from program or finance staff, and in all cases the grant professional should seek final approval from them before submitting the template to the foundation.

A variety of books and online resources are available for those wanting to learn about creating budgets (1). For the purposes of our discussion, it is sufficient to mention that (a) all relevant expenses including staff time and benefits must be included in even the most simplistic of budgets, (b) costs should ideally be allocated across programs and functions for a more realistic budget, and (c) revenues such as grants, earned income such as program fees, and in-kind donations should also be included in the budget for a more comprehensive picture.

# Addressing Challenging Issues

Several types of organizations face challenges when applying to funders, based on internal or external issues as well as due to their intrinsic nature. For example, very large institutions such as universities or hospitals as well as small, grassroots organizations are subject to strict scrutiny by prospective funders based on their size and management structure. As with any nonprofit, the best course of action is to identify and answer any potential questions proactively, taking input from senior staff, program heads, and grant professionals. The team approach to designing programs as described in Chapter 3 presents the best opportunity to determine red flags in funders' minds; for large organizations, it may be the existence of enormous endowments, extensive donor pools, or countless development staff members raising money through a variety of sources.

Understanding the obstacles to being funded can go a long way in helping create more effective grant proposals. Grant professionals should communicate with local grant makers, especially those that may have rejected previous proposals by the organization, and discover some of their valid concerns. These challenges can then be discussed with appropriate staff and volunteers and responses can be developed for future conversations, proposals, and site visits. The grant proposals of such organizations in particular should address these concerns in the appropriate sections, or an FAQ-style document can be attached in the appendices.

Perceptions can be damaging for nonprofit funding as well. Foundations typically view very small, grassroots and faith-based organizations as unprofessional or lacking, based on their characteristics and nontraditional ways of doing business. Grassroots organizations, for instance, are perceived as being ineffective or inefficient; such organizations should attempt to dispel funder concerns by explaining their unique management structures and governance procedures. Like other nonprofits, grassroots nonprofits should also focus on community support and show a variety of funding streams before seeking foundation grants. These efforts can go a long way in increasing their chances of success. Similarly, start-up and smaller faith-based organizations are perceived as having little or no accountability. Some issues that both types of organizations should address in their grant proposals are governance, outcomes, stability, and sustainability.

In addition, faith-based organizations of all sizes should discuss their process of ensuring equal opportunity and community involvement beyond religious members. They should also focus on their strategic planning, bring in secular advisors or board members, and broaden their constituency. Further, since the mission and vision statements of faith-based groups typically depict their religious nature, it is important somewhere in their grant proposals to include language and information assuring nondiscrimination. Secular funders in particular want to know whether the policies of equal opportunity and nondiscrimination are indeed being followed in spirit as well. Lutheran Social Services in Austin, TX, has a powerfully faith-based mission statement of "providing help, healing, and hope in the name of Jesus Christ" but their proposals and other materials state clearly that "all services are provided without regard to religion, race, and gender" and often explain that "75% or more of the 35,000 persons served annually are non-Lutheran." Additionally, their values statement includes assertions about providing high quality care, setting standards, remaining relevant and accountable, and being good stewards. Thirdly, they offer evidence of their nondiscriminatory nature through mention of accreditations and awards by external agencies.

At various times during their existence, nonprofits face a number of difficult situations and issues that may pose obstacles to funding. Apart from intrinsic issues discussed above, these may also relate to some sort of

---

## Funder Perspective: Marion and Henry Knott Foundation
*Greg Cantori, Executive Director*

Q: How can faith-based organizations convince potential funders that they are a good investment?

A: It's nice to know if an organization it is faith-based, but what is more important is that it should have good management, good programs, and good directors. The fact that an applicant is faith-based is just icing on the cake, because it tells us that there is passion behind the work. At the same time, we are very critical when we look at these organizations because these days many so called faith-based groups are fly by night operations, looking to line their own pockets. So we are very careful and critique all in that regard. My advice to faith-based nonprofits when approaching foundations is to look at the foundation's mission; if the foundation is religion-based then focus on that, but if the foundation is secular then played the faith-based aspect down and focus on core competencies. Also, our own trustees are not excited about intruding scripture in the programs, even though our foundation has a catholic mission. As an example, lots of homeless shelters require people to sit for service before eating. Obviously, the homeless are not all catholic, or even Christian, but they have no choice but to participate in the service. Sometimes the dining room leads through the chapel. I feel that this is unconscionable, and we as a foundation stay away from that. It is very important for a nonprofit to put the needs of the client first and foremost, and this practice reminds me too much of old school missionary work.

negative publicity, crisis, a dramatic decrease in numbers served, or any other situation that funders may be concerned about. As touched upon in Chapter 2, in any such matter it is best to remain in constant communication with all stakeholders including current and potential donors. This ensures that funders not only understand the true reasons for the problems, but are also made fully aware of the organization's plans for rectification or future improvement. The grant proposal itself should address the issue in question seriously and honestly, and any follow-up concerns by funders should be handled by the organization's senior staff.

Further, ethical considerations for grant professionals center on providing true and accurate information to funders regarding a myriad of topics: services, sustainability, resource allocation, and most importantly numbers served. Grant consultants who are not involved in the everyday operations of their clients should remain doubly vigilant to ensure that they are representing organizations that remain true to their mission and conduct all activities in an honest manner. In a nutshell, the grant proposal is more than just a collection of the facts—it is a reflection of the entire organization and its people.

## ENDNOTES

(1) See List of Suggested Resources.

# Chapter 7 Checklist

## Organizational Readiness

| Indicator | Status |
|---|---|
| Do we have a case statement for our organization? | |
| Are senior staff and board members involved in addressing questions of strategic concern for the purposes of our grant proposals? | |
| Do our proposals adequately explain key issues of sustainability and financial stability from a holistic viewpoint? | |
| Are we aware of specific funder concerns—both actual and perceived—about our organization and do we have a plan to address them? | |

## Grant Professional Readiness

| Indicator | Status |
|---|---|
| Do I have master proposals or templates of proposals that are submitted more frequently to funders? | |
| Do my proposals typically contain an executive summary even if not required by the funder? | |
| Do my proposals adequately explain the need for our programs and services through the use of both statistical and human information? | |
| Do my proposals discuss my organization's competitive advantage without badmouthing my competitors? | |
| Do my proposals include a timeline for implementation and key staff qualifications? | |
| Do my proposals include a section on outcome measurement? | |
| Do my proposals address the issue of sustainability and financial stability? | |

## Part III

# While the Jury's Out

# Produce Fabulous Site Visits

*"For a nonprofit, preparing for a site visit can be very helpful because it presents an opportunity to think about what they are doing and a chance to tell their story in a comprehensive way by involving as many people as possible. If you see it as an opportunity to sit down as a group and discuss where you are, then it becomes a reality test. You can assess all the work you have done, the weaknesses that may be present, and ways to improve yourself. It allows you to ground yourself as an organization."*

Victor De Luca, President
Jessie Smith Noyes Foundation

Nonprofit organizations frequently have a love–hate relationship with funder site visits; the main reason being that the process tends to be cloaked in secrecy and that visitors are viewed as having the upper hand. At the same time, there is also the realization that site visits are a necessity that may signal a grant maker's interest in moving forward and seeking more information than has been provided in the initial grant proposal: a definite indication of the possibility of being funded. As a result of these conflicting emotions and a lack of time and resources available to many nonprofit staff and leadership, the site visit is often reduced to a tour or a meeting, rather than a dynamic opportunity to demonstrate programs and clients in action and lend a more compelling face to the organization. By understanding the reasons behind a typical site visit and devising creative alternatives to a seemingly mundane event, grant professionals and other staff can ensure that their grant proposals get the needed boost to be approved, and their organization's image in funders' eyes is further enhanced.

# The Rationale

Once the grant application has been submitted, the waiting can become excruciating, especially if a foundation typically takes months to respond. During this stage of the grant seeking process, many organizations are subjected to pre-grant site visits. Although not mandatory, this practice is on the increase because of a higher number of equally deserving applicants and fewer funding resources to distribute among them. More importantly, as funders begin to appreciate the value of becoming more accessible and in tune with community needs, site visits can develop into an avenue for relationship building.

The fact that site visits assist in making grant decisions cannot be denied. The findings of our research show that a correlation exists between successful site visits and grants: 67% of respondents reported that no grants were denied after a site visit, and 22.4% reported that only 25% of grants were denied after a site visit (see Figure 8.1).

Foundations that do conduct site visits prior to making funding decisions take these events very seriously for a variety of reasons; nonprofit staff that can fully grasp these reasons can take full advantage of an upcoming site visit to satisfy the needs of the visitors. Keep in mind that if a site visit has been requested, it implies that the applicant organization has made at least the first cut and is being reviewed more deeply. Some of the possible reasons why a site visit may be conducted are as follows:

- When the programs or services of an organization are complex or extensive, viewing them in action may be the only way for a foundation official to understand operations.

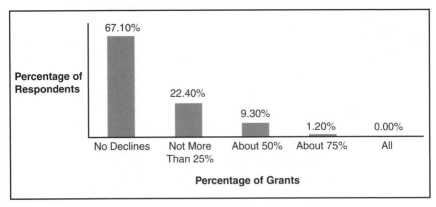

Figure 8.1  *Grants Funded After Site Visit*

- New or innovative programs may require a site visit to understand them in the context of the entire organization.

- Start-up organizations or first-time applicants may not have any credibility or name recognition until further investigation during a site visit reveals how they do business.

- When multiple applicants provide similar services, a site visit may highlight differences and help the funder determine which is more deserving.

- In the case of capital requests, funders may want to obtain a more tangible perspective of the project or equipment than is possible on paper. Similarly, when being asked to support emergency requests such a leaking roof or disaster-related expenses, funders may wish to witness the damage before making a commitment.

- In the case of operating requests, funders may want to see the impact of their operating dollars on administration, facilities, and other everyday needs.

- In the case of collaborative proposals, foundations may want to meet with all partners in one location, ask specific questions about the project, and observe group dynamics.

- Some funders may wish to meet with clients to understand their needs and the impact of the applicant organization's services on them.

- Funders who take nonprofit personnel qualifications into account when making funding decisions may find it beneficial to personally meet staff and volunteers in order to assess this key indicator of success.

- Some foundation officials may have specific questions that were not addressed in the applicant's grant proposal or may want to verify certain issues they feel strongly about.

- Foundation officers and trustees who consider it essential to build relationships with grantees may want to meet them face-to-face and observe them in action before making an investment.

- Some foundations encourage their trustees or donors to attend site visits in order to improve their level of involvement in the nonprofit community, increase their passion for specific causes, or show them how their investment is being utilized.

Although other individual reasons for site visits may exist, the ones listed above are sufficient as a means of grasping the most basic motivations of grant makers. Once these motivations are understood, grant professionals together with other staff and leaders of the organization can design a well-planned site visit that addresses concerns, enhances the grant proposal, and increases the chances of getting funded.

# The Preparations

At many organizations, the grant professional's involvement in grant seeking ends with the submittal of the proposal, or at least takes a hiatus until the funder's decision is announced. Typically, the news of a site visit is sent by the foundation directly to the executive director or CEO, whose responsibility then becomes to assemble a team and prepare for the event. In an environment where interdepartmental corporation for the sake of grant seeking does not exist, the grant professional may be the last person to be notified of the visit, and he or she may not be invited to participate in the preparations. However, as the person with the most in-depth knowledge of the funder, as well as the information provided in the proposal, the grant professional can be an asset to the organization preparing for a site visit.

The basic steps to follow when informed of an impending site visit are as follows:

1. Don't panic: many staff members feel intensely pressured at the thought of having an outsider witness their activities, especially one who makes funding decisions. Organizational leaders may feel inadequate and want to spend money on unnecessary preparations, facility adornment, etc. The best way to deal with this panic at an organizational level is for the grant professional to explain some of the possible reasons of the visit and to educate everyone about the positive consequences of a successful visit.

2. Assemble a "site visit team" to plan and implement the site visit from beginning to end, including follow-up. For operating and program requests, this team should consist of the grant professional, the development director, one or more program leaders, the heads of finance and administration, the executive director, and the board chair. For capital requests, the chair of the campaign committee and key capital campaign staff should be a part of the team as well. If the request included collaborators in a significant capacity, representatives from those agencies should also be included. Other people may be involved in the team from time to time as needed, but those mentioned above will become the core team members whose input and effort will be instrumental in the success of the site visit.

3. Hold an initial team meeting in person or over the phone to inform everyone of the date and time of the site visit, plan the team's activities going forward, and assign responsibilities to team members. A team leader should be selected—ideally this should not be the executive director or board chair, since they have other more pressing tasks. The grant professional may take the lead in this capacity if agreed upon by everyone.

4. Contact the foundation to ask additional questions about the purpose and nature of the site visit. Many times a site visit is unsuccessful, or at least uninspiring, because of a lack of information provided by foundation staff; further, most visitors will not give details of the site visit beforehand until requested to do so, although some larger foundations do send an agenda or other information prior to visiting. During this conversation with the foundation, the team leader should explain that the purpose of their questions is to ensure that the organization is prepared to conduct the site visit in a manner that would be meaningful and useful for the foundation as they make their funding decisions.

   - How long will the site visit last? This will help plan the format and the amount of information that can be easily presented. Knowing the length of the visit also helps in understanding the basic reasons for the site visit; a half-hour site visit may only be a formality while a half-day site visit may imply that the funder is looking for a serious conversation to help in decision-making.

   - Who will attend? Knowing in advance if any trustees or donors will be attending allows for prospect research and ensures that counterparts from the nonprofit's board are also present. For example, if a trustee who is a medical doctor and donates to a number of arts organizations plans to attend the site visit, the site visit could stress the arts education component of the organization and any board members who are in the medical field could attend the visit.

   - Do you have an agenda or format in mind, or will you have one at a later date? If the answer is no, permission should be sought to create a format and agenda and send it to the foundation official before the site visit. This shows a high level of professionalism and a respect for the visitors' time, while reducing the site visit team's stress.

   - What is the main reason for the site visit? Although the answer may be vague and generalized, such as "we always conduct site visits as part of the grant making process," some foundation officials may be open to sharing other reasons. The team leader should ask if any specific issues from the grant proposal need to be addressed or if any other aspect of the organization is of particular concern to the foundation.

   - Is any specific person, information, or document required during the site visit? Many times visitors will ask for detailed financials or request to meet with a staff or volunteer who may not be present, thereby causing undue stress to the organization. Knowing this information in advance can result in a smoothly run site visit.

5. Conduct one or more subsequent team meetings. These meetings will allow for planning of the site visit format (this process will be

dealt with in detail in the next section) and reviewing the original proposal submitted to the funder to gain team members' feedback about areas requiring further clarification.

6. Debrief and follow-up, including a discussion of lessons learned and ways to improve future site visits.

---

## Funder Perspective: Jessie Smith Noyes Foundation

*Victor De Luca, President*

Q: What do you look for when conducting a site visit?
A: The important thing for us in a site visit is to be authentic. You can tell who are the folks who are grounded and who are just putting on a show. When you walk into a room, right away you can pick up vibes of how people relate to each other and the volume of work that occurs there. For us, leadership development, particularly secondary leadership, is very important. We want to see the people in the organization other than the director—what their level of interaction with each other is, what they are capable of and what their level of knowledge is. Is only one person speaking or is everyone? If the director says that member organizations are important to us, but if only one person is speaking, that doesn't seem like a culture of engagement or collaboration. Usually, it is very easy to tell who the decision maker is.

It is also telling whether you even meet with the board of directors or not. At one site visit which took an entire day, I met with the executive director in the morning and then she scheduled meetings with different people throughout the day; the next time I met her was in the evening. This was a very rewarding experience because it showed that she believed in her staff and not just in her own leadership. We also conduct some site visits in our own offices, where we have groups come meet us in New York, but that is not as effective because it is a different feel walking down the street or visiting a community center—it's the intangibles we want to take in. It's all about storytelling. We fund stories and the people who tell them. Obviously the numbers are important, but in reality they are the "gravy" of the story.

Thirdly, an organization should practice what it preaches. If it is a "progressive" organization, then is it also progressive in its workplace? If you promise diversity in your mission, but when we walk in everyone in the room is white or male, it allows us to ask a whole set of questions that we wouldn't otherwise even think to ask. Also, don't be ashamed of who you are or where you are located. Don't treat foundation folk differently just because we come from a big city.

# The Format

Site visits can have numerous formats, ranging from meetings to presentations to tours, depending on the capacity and resources of the organization, the time allotted for the visit, and the creativity of the site visit team. Many organizations are further hindered by circumstances related to their work, such as confidentiality issues or the absence of physical facilities. In any case, the site visit team can make the best possible effort to create a successful site visit by preparing and practicing the format in advance.

Although some consider them boring, face-to-face meetings are essential to some site visits. The visitors may want to ask specific questions related to finance or programs that are best dealt with in an office environment with the least distractions. The foundation may also favor the meetings format because of its own culture and preference. However, this format tends to make the site visit forgettable and unemotional, negating the entire purpose of a site visit as an enhancement of the grant proposal that motivates the funder to give. Unless absolutely necessary, meetings should be avoided or should form only the smallest portion of the site visit.

If the meeting-type format becomes necessary because of funder preference or due to limitations of the organization itself, some creative elements can be introduced to ensure that the visitors leave inspired rather than indifferent. One such element is ambiance: the meeting room may have pictures of clients or framed letters on the walls, handiwork by student artists on the side tables, or other such interesting pieces that may prompt conversation or give an emotional touch to an otherwise dry discussion. Two other elements are content and audience selection, which will be explained later in the chapter.

A tour is also a popular site visit format, although organizations utilize it more for capital campaigns than for other types of grant requests. This does not imply that site visits for capital campaigns are any easier to conduct: many visitors have difficulty visualizing buildings, exhibits, or programs where empty space currently exists. Although materials such as architectural drawings and visual depictions help, the key to success is a tour that is well-organized and conducted by a person with not only extensive knowledge of the campaign but also an emotional connection—the founder for example.

Many visitors themselves request a tour, especially if the applicant is an academic institution, museum, health center, or the like. Tours are a wonderful opportunity to showcase operations and meet clients and volunteers, as long as there is plenty to see. If students are being trained, patients treated, or experiments conducted, nonprofits should make every effort to bring in visitors, even if just for a few minutes. If confidentiality issues form a potential obstacle, a private viewing area along with prior signing of waivers may be helpful, for instance during one-on-one mentoring with at-risk youth, domestic violence counseling sessions, or the like.

Unfortunately for some organizations, services are not performed at their physical location, for example, in mentoring organizations where students and volunteers meet in schools or arts organizations where plays are held in community centers or other locations. Some organizations may find that funders are willing to conduct site visits after-hours or accompany staff and volunteers to service locations if possible. It is the responsibility of the site visit team to offer this alternative in advance and suggest possible ways to witness programs or meet with clients externally.

Online tours are also gaining popularity, especially for capital campaigns but easily adaptable for other types of grant requests as well. The Foss Waterway Seaport in Tacoma, WA, uploaded not only concept drawings to their website but also an interactive interior concept plan with numbers that reveal details about key features when the mouse pointer is run over them. Although the main target audience of virtual tours and online photo galleries is individual donors, an organization can also invite foundation staff and trustees to take advantage of these tools in order to gain further information about them. Textual, audio, or video testimonials on the website can be a creative alternative to meeting clients in person, especially if confidentiality issues exist or clients are not available during a specific site visit to meet with funders. Minnesota Teen Challenge has several videos on its website for those interested in hearing firsthand about the work of the organization and their effect on clients; visitors can view student testimonials, graduate videos, and much more.

Oftentimes, international organizations seeking support in the United States face a unique difficulty in conducting site visits: foundations tend to be unsure about the appropriate use of their funds and the impact of their support. Project Hope conducts "delegation visits" consisting of 72 hours on the ground on location, when visitors get the opportunity to interact with field staff, beneficiaries, local doctors and administrators, and government officials. As a result, visitors not only observe programmatic work but also gain an understanding of the health issues in that particular country or region. Apart from potential donors, other people invited to participate in these visits include partner organizations and private funders interested in that country or issue.

While a large number of organizations do not fall in the same category as Project Hope, it is possible to implement some elements of these delegation visits into their own format, for example, creating specialized visits that last longer than a typical site visit and involve a discussion of issues as well as programs and services. Holden Village, an ecumenical retreat center in a remote area of Washington, possesses a history of hospitality that is inculcated in site visits. When the bus bringing the visitors arrives, a greeting party consisting of staff and guests currently staying at Holden Village welcomes the visitors. Because of the isolated location of the organization and the fact that only one boat is available per day, all site visits are overnight. Visitors experience every unique aspect of Holden Village during their stay, including activities, worship, and a tour of the village and surrounding areas. Astonishingly, officials from a variety of foundations have stayed overnight at the retreat and enjoyed their stay.

Moving a step beyond the tour—where the visitor is a bystander—some organizations are courageous enough to conduct participatory site visits, where visitors are directly involved in the programs and services offered and interact directly with clients. At the lowest level of this spectrum are organizations that allow visitors to accompany staff during their everyday activities; take the example of the Maternity Care Coalition in Philadelphia, PA, whose site visits are particularly moving because prospective funders are driven out in one of their MOMobile® vans to visit impoverished and at-risk mothers. Accompanying them on these trips are community health workers who support the client mothers. These trips allow visitors to meet clients, highlighting constituent needs and shedding light on how the staff interacts with them.

At the other end of the spectrum is Roca in Chelsea, MA, where funders have the opportunity to participate in an important and unique part of the program: peacemaking circles. This approach involves participants sitting in a circle, speaking honestly, listening to each other respectfully, and taking turns speaking. Each person speaks only when holding an object that is passed clockwise (in the direction of the sun's movement) from one participant to the next. The feedback received from funders is positive, as they not only enjoy the experience but learn a great deal from and about Roca's clients.

Many different types of nonprofits can implement a participatory site visit by analyzing their operations and determining if any aspects are conducive to involvement by an outsider with little or no training. At a learning center, a visitor may be asked to become the teacher's assistant, while at a food bank he or she may be requested to hand out meals to homeless clients. Before making preparations, however, it is important to seek the funder's permission or at least notify them that their participation will be requested during the site visit.

The optimum format for a site visit is a combination of several formats, created by borrowing techniques from donor cultivation while keeping in mind the unique nature of the grant funder's needs and expectations. An ideal combination format (if the visitors have left it completely to the discretion of the host) would be as follows:

1. Five minute meet-and-greet with informal introductions.
2. Short video presentation with testimonials by a couple of clients and/or volunteers and an overall view of the organization touching on history, programs, and major accomplishments.

3. Designated speaker (may be the founder, board chair, or executive director) officially welcomes the visitors and makes a 10-second introduction of all attendees. He or she then talks about the organization in more detail and uses a PowerPoint presentation to highlight key areas as mentioned in the grant proposal. The timing of this section depends on overall site visit length and may be divided into presentations by two people: one to offer a more inspirational overview of the organization and the other to explain the proposal details.

4. Handouts, folders, or other materials are circulated and if necessary some indication of what they contain is given by the designated speaker. Unless critical to the previous presentations, handouts should not be given out earlier because they tend to distract the listeners.

5. If a tour is possible—or in the case of a capital campaign, necessary—visitors are requested to accompany one or two organizational representatives *only*. The tour should not make up more than 50% of the entire site visit length: in many cases it should be even less. The tour should be geared towards the request: for operating expense proposals visitors should be able to see the facility and meet clients and volunteers, while for program requests they should be able to witness the program in action and meet with program staff.

6. Visitors are led back to the meeting room to meet with key staff members such as the executive director, board chair and program directors. The floor should be opened to the visitors to ask questions and address any issues of concern. Alternatively, if more time is available, the visitors may meet with staff and board members separately in their offices.

In this, as with all other aspects of grant seeking, various departments within and outside of fundraising must work together. Prospect research should be conducted to learn as much as possible about the visiting foundation's history of giving (or not giving) and its interests and capabilities. Major gifts and annual fund officers should recommend donors or other key stakeholders who may be invited to attend the site visit; program staff should do the same from a programmatic perspective by recommending clients who speak well or volunteers who have been with the organization for a number of years. Special event staff should share strategies for event administration and management, including any presentations or print materials that can be effectively used during the site visit. The marketing staff should similarly contribute video clips, recorded testimonials, and other marketing materials that may be available. Finally, site visits are a good opportunity for staff and board members to work together and may serve as further engagement for high level volunteers.

## Funder Perspective: Orange County Community Foundation

*Todd Hanson, Vice-President of Donor Relations and Programs*

The best site visits are ones in which the agency is able to give you a good sense about the work they are doing and why it is important. For example, at one organization we met several clients and observed them going through the program. This gave us such a good understanding of what they were doing that I went back a second time and took a few donors with me. On the other hand, another organization focused solely on a building they recently completed but didn't tie that back into the services they were providing; that was a missed opportunity to reinforce the value of the services they provide.

DO:
• have a board member present and participating
• provide concrete stories related to your work
• give a synopsis of your request
• be prepared and have a format
• quantify how the money will be used: even though we know operating funds are essential for you, donors want to see what they are supporting

DON'T:
• give false or misleading information such as "we are the only organization providing this service"
• criticize other organizations

# The Content

It is almost impossible to teach an organization about the ideal information or content to present during a site visit. However, keeping in mind the basic reasons for a typical site visit explained in the beginning of this chapter, it is possible to discuss what may be critical content for a site visit. The site visit team should use the discussion below to determine the best fit with their organization and proposal.

A major motive to conduct a site visit is for the funder to observe programs in action. As mentioned in previous sections, tours and testimonials are an excellent way to show some program aspects in a positive and real light, as opposed to the flat explanations given on paper. Visitors may ask for—or expect to better understand—processes such as intake, case management, and outcome measurement; staff composition reflecting the ethnic and gender makeup of their clients or communities is another important piece of the puzzle. Having program documents on hand is also a good idea, in case a question arises about how a specific activity is conducted. If the organization offers a service or program that is similar to others in the community, program staff must be prepared to give an explanation or description of how theirs is different or superior. In fact, this issue should form a key component of the site visit content regardless of whether it is asked by a visitor or not.

Funders also conduct site visits to view the organization's facility and offices, including location in relation to clients. Although funders are aware and understanding of the fact that nonprofit facilities tend to be less attractive or ostentatious than their corporate counterparts, visitors will take notice of damage, disrepair, or substandard workplaces. They will also look at the degree to which the environment is appropriate to client needs, for example, a day care center with little natural light and no pictures on the walls is bound to leave a negative impression and plenty of questions in the visitors' minds. Staff must be prepared to explain the reasons for any obvious and unnecessarily pitiable working conditions such as torn carpeting, lack of room for program staff, and the like. It is important in these cases to tell the truth and explain why finances may not be available to improve conditions: a perfect opportunity to bring home the need for the visitor's investment. As always, any discussions of facilities or operating expenses must always tie back to the clients and programs.

Additionally, organizations should expect their people to be judged during a site visit. This includes higher level staff as well as volunteers and front line program staff. Visitors want to not only see how staff works together, but they also look for indications of leadership and communication styles. They may ask penetrating questions related to programming in order to assess the qualifications and knowledge of key personnel or they may ask about staff turnover and volunteer dependence. They will most probably want to talk to the executive director in private to gauge his or her attitude and expertise. In addition, visitors almost always want to obtain details about board involvement and the relationship of board members with administration. All possible types of documents and information related to the personnel aspect should be on hand during the site visit; this includes statistics about staff and board composition, leadership committee descriptions, and board giving histories.

Another critical issue most site visits address is the nonprofit's finances, since funders use current financial performance and future viability in making funding decisions. Visitors will typically ask questions or seek documents related to the operating and/or program budgets, year-end financial statements, salaries, earned income, and various grant awards. Other questions may deal with loans, rent or mortgage payments, and the ratio of programs to fundraising–administrative expenses. The person in charge of accounting and finance must remain one of the key members of the site visit team as well as a major participant during the visit in order to answer any financial questions that may arise (see Figure 8.2).

Related to the content of the site visit is another important but often under-utilized aspect of the site visit: choosing the attendees or participants. Many site visits turn mundane because they involve only the organization's main personnel or because other attendees are mere onlookers; it also shows a lack

---

Organization: _____

Date of Visit: _____

Amount of Request: $_____

Programs:
Does the program or organization sufficiently meet the needs of the community?
What other organizations are doing similar work in the community and is there any collaboration?
What are some challenges faced by the organization?
What were the perceptions about clients, their stories, and needs?

Facilities:
What were the perceptions about the environment and working conditions?
Is there sufficient technical and physical infrastructure to meet needs and/or to expand?

Personnel:
Is the agency's leadership well-qualified to achieve success?
Did the program staff have adequate knowledge of programs and clients?
What was the overall impression of the interaction between staff, leadership, and clients?

Finances:
Does the organization seem financially sound?
What are some possible red flags that need further clarification?

Other:
What are the organization's strengths and weaknesses?

Comments:

_____

Recommendations:

_____

---

Figure 8.2 *Sample Site Visit Evaluation Checklist*

of interest or respect on the part of the host if only lower level employees attend. Funders agree that site visits should include board members (surprisingly, many organizations are unable to convince their board to attend) and any collaborating organization's leadership. For organizations struggling with inactive or uninvolved boards, a site visit may present the perfect opportunity to motivate and inspire them by giving them roles of responsibility: the designated speaker, host in charge of making introductions, or the like. Although there is no magic number of maximum participants, having one to three board members and the same number of clients/volunteers is usually considered acceptable. This number also depends on the size of the meeting room and the length of the site visit. Also, if a combination visit format is being used, fewer people can attend each portion of the site visit in order to give more the opportunity to participate; one client may attend the presentation while another may lead the tour or program directors may be absent from the presentation if they have meetings scheduled with the visitors later during the visit. Reality is sometimes very different, however. According to our research, the largest portion of responding nonprofits (84.1%) requires senior staff to attend site visits, while less than half (37.2%) of organizations have board members attending these important events (see Figure 8.3).

Generally speaking, clients, volunteers, and even lower level staff members can transform a site visit from boring to inspiring, as long as they are contributing to the visit either by speaking or even by just performing host duties such as

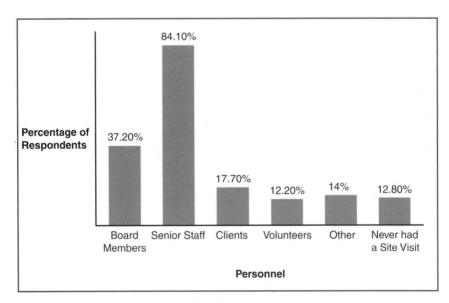

Figure 8.3 *Personnel Attending Site Visits*

welcoming visitors and answering questions. They may also become active participants in conducting all or part of the site visit. For instance, Lutheran Social Services in Austin, TX, asks the girls in their residential treatment program to lead tours and share their stories. In return, the girls get "points" for participating in the site visit as they improve their social skills. Similarly, Teen Lifeline in Phoenix, AZ, utilizes teen volunteers in site visits outside of hotline hours, showing how they operate the hotline and conducting tours. Because teenagers are not only the agency's volunteers but potential clients as well, they are able to give funders a unique perspective and bring home the organization's impact.

Regardless of who participates, it is important to prepare all the components of the site visit in advance, especially if a combination format will be utilized. Scripts and talking points are one way to ensure that all the relevant information is provided and no glaring mistakes are made. If clients or volunteers are speaking, practicing a script or tour route becomes even more necessary. Additionally, as mentioned earlier, a team review of the grant proposal that was originally submitted to the visitors is also essential in order to remind all participants of the promises and requests made. Not only may the grant professional have forgotten what he or she wrote, but program staff or the executive director may not be aware of its content at all. Further, since proposals usually include dated information like the previous fiscal year's numbers, program and finance staff should be asked to prepare the latest information regarding their areas of responsibility.

Other ways to prepare include testing all technical equipment in advance and having a staff member on hand during the visit to correct any audio or video difficulties. Also, care must be taken to ensure that the date and time of the site visit is ideal—when clients can be available or when programs are in session. If the visitors have specified a date and time which is not conducive to a high-quality visit, they should be asked to consider some alternative times; typically, funders understand such requests because their aim is to experience the programs and meet the recipients of their funds.

From the nonprofit perspective, an upcoming site visit should be reason to celebrate, rather than a cause of concern. It is an opportunity to present the real face of the organization by placing emphasis on the people served, their stories, challenges, and successes. It offers a tangible and emotional alternative to a two-dimensional grant proposal that may not be sufficient no matter how skilled the grant writer is. Although one hopes that a successful site visit will ultimately lead to funding, the holistic grant seeking approach recommended by this book celebrates the site visit as much more: a means of internal improvements such as board engagement and program enhancement, as well as a vehicle for external strategies such as public relations within the community and relationship building with grant makers. Once an organization views the site visit in this light, all departments, personnel, and volunteers will automatically become involved in preparing for it and ensuring its success.

# Chapter 8 Checklist

## Organizational Readiness

| Indicator | Status |
| --- | --- |
| Do all staff and board members understand the importance and value of pre-grant site visits? | |
| Do we have a site visit team that includes the grants department for site visits preparation? | |
| Do our board members attend site visits? | |
| Do our site visits offer a combination of tours, meetings, and presentations that utilize donor cultivation techniques for maximum impact? | |
| Do we make various staff and volunteers available to funders during site visits to answer questions and address concerns? | |
| Are site visits viewed by staff and volunteers as a means of board engagement, program enhancement, and public relations? | |

## Grant Professional Readiness

| Indicator | Status |
| --- | --- |
| Have I communicated the importance and value of pre-grant site visits to my leadership and staff members? | |
| Am I involved in site visit preparations by offering my time and expertise? | |
| Have I informed my leadership and others attending site visits about the grant proposal in question and any funder preferences? | |

Part IV

# After the Grant Award

# Chapter 9

# Steward Funds With Integrity

*"Just as an organization has a stewardship strategy with individual donors, it is important to have a plan for maintaining relationships with foundations. For our foundation, we do like to get an occasional e-mail that gives us an update on the program we supported or just an update on a recent accomplishment of the agency. It is also appropriate to periodically request a site visit or a meeting with a foundation. They may decline, but making the offer is helpful."*

Todd M. Hanson, Vice-President of Donor Relations and Programs
Orange County Community Foundation

The day when an acceptance letter from a foundation arrives in the mail is a day of celebration, regardless of how large the organization or how small the award. It signals a victory for not only the grant professional who wrote the proposal but also for the program staff who are relying on the funds and the board members who are hoping for a relationship with a local funder. Regrettably, many nonprofits—especially smaller ones—consider this the last step in the grant seeking process, and once a thank you letter is sent back, the grant and all the effort put in during proposal writing is already ancient history. Even larger organizations and those with more professional staff members sometimes fail to take into account the new chapter that has now begun: grant management. Others are unsuccessful in translating individual and major gift stewardship activities to foundation grants, leaving many opportunities for further relationship building on the table. By realizing that stewardship is in reality a two-pronged approach that melds internal grant management with external reporting to funders, the organization can gain strategic advantages in seeking and managing grant awards in the long run.

# Foundation Grant Management

Grant management is typically not considered a part of stewardship, and is often delegated to the finance department as a strictly internal process; further, grant professionals are oftentimes not involved in post-award activities. However, the truth is that managing a grant award as promised and complying with all the possible regulations is the most important, albeit the least glamorous, aspect of exceptional stewardship and therefore of grant seeking in general. It is also the most difficult component of stewardship because it requires interdepartmental cooperation and a reliance on program staff who may already be overwhelmed with their daily responsibilities. For this reason, a quick overview of the grant management process (as it relates to nongovernmental grant awards) is provided below so that grant professionals can better understand and implement the principles of grant management across the organization.

Organizations that receive a grant from a government agency quickly become aware of post-award grant management practices, as required by the law and the funding entity. A host of conditions, practices, and procedures must be put into place for these types of awards, leaving the grant recipient with no choice but to learn the process and abide by the rules. On the other hand, organizations that typically do not receive government monies may not be as particular about implementing grant management practices for foundation grants, mainly because the award letter does not arrive with a packet of instructions and guidelines. Additionally, some organizations receiving government funds tend to keep the grant management policies and procedures for those grants separate from private grants, although many of the practices can be shared or at least learned from.

Foundation grants may not require the same level of post-award management, but they certainly deserve some sort of management to ensure that promises are kept, reports submitted on time, and funders appropriately recognized. In today's funding climate, grant professionals are becoming more aware of their role in grants management; while in many larger nonprofits, the grant management function is separate from the grant writing function. This chapter will discuss how these two areas of responsibility can work together and even be performed by the same person.

In order to create the best setup for foundation grant management, the grant professional should examine the grant's function within the organization. This examination should take into account the number of proposal writers and the degree of overlap between the job functions of grant writers, grant managers, and grant administrators. In many organizations—especially smaller ones—the same person is responsible for all three areas of responsibility, while in others, program staff act as grant managers. Although this job overlap, or the lack thereof, usually depends on the resources available to the organization to hire additional staff, many times it is also an outcome of the type of grants typically being received by the organization. If only small grant awards are the norm, or if none of the grants awarded have extensive reporting requirements, the grant writer will typically act as grant administrator, providing not only writing services but also coordinating award implementation and ensuring grant compliance.

At the risk of sounding repetitive, a grant management team is a better practice in many cases than a single grant administrator or grant manager not only by ensuring that the work gets completed in a timely manner but also by creating a system of checks and balances. The people involved in this team should include the grant writer, the director of finance and/or accounting, the overall head of programs, and the director of the department(s) who will be using the grant funds. In the case of specific campaigns or grants for particular projects, the people supervising them should also be included in the team, such as human resources, facilities, and the like. The team should be assembled and coached as early as possible, rather than at the time a grant is received. One way to conduct ongoing team building is to establish formal rules and regulations guiding the team's functions through discussions and documentation.

As part of this documentation, a grant management manual should be compiled early on by the team, highlighting the main processes and procedures to be used during the term of the award. At smaller organizations, or those focusing exclusively on nongovernment grants, this manual can be a simple document with the sole purpose of guiding team members through the compliance process and explaining the roles and duties of each team member. At large institutions, especially academic institutions, this manual usually takes the form of extensive documentation of each and every aspect of proposal writing, submission, reporting, and compliance activities. As mentioned earlier, this chapter focuses on foundation funding, which tends to be more simplistic in nature, although not any less important.

When a grant award notification is received, the team should quickly assemble to examine the requirements of the award and establish a management process for it. The initial steps for the team include:

1. Reading the award package and making note of any important items such as restrictions, due dates, matching fund requirements, and follow-up procedures.

2. Informing key internal and external stakeholders of the grant award; further details are given in the stewardship section of this chapter.

3. Reviewing the grant application to remind the grant professional and program staff about the outcomes or activities promised and the budgets submitted.

4. Determining the roles and responsibilities of team members as well as others outside the team, including volunteers and collaborating agency staff.

5. Discussing issues pertaining to grant management, compliance, and reporting:

   • The funder's reporting requirements and how well they match the existing evaluation methods used by the organization. The team should ensure that all members are aware of the requirements and determine if any major obstacles may be faced in the collection of data.

   • The process for making any changes to the scope of work or services if needed, and the necessary approval process to follow from a program perspective as well as for the purposes of book-keeping.

Grant professionals may find it beneficial to create a summary sheet (also called a deliverables list) of the grant award and distribute it among all team members, especially program staff, either in print or electronic format for periodic review. It is also helpful to obtain signatures from key people responsible for reporting and compliance, so that accountability is shared among the entire team and deadlines are followed (see Figure 9.1).

All those responsible for spending grant funds must be well-informed about the entire grant management and accounting process, and part of the team effort includes the creation of a grants management plan involving finance and accounting staff. These personnel can provide training—whether in person, via email, or through the manual described earlier—to program staff on pertinent financial concepts such as allowable expenses, direct versus indirect costs, how to allocate funds, what the grant money can be used for, how to seek permission before making purchases, and much more. It is important to involve the finance department from the beginning so that program staff is aware of the practices they have to follow and the forms they are required to complete.

Although accounting practices differ among organizations, most finance departments follow similar procedures for grant management. Instead of assuming that this is indeed the case, however, the grant management team

Requested Amount: $50,000                    Granted Amount: $40,000
Grantee: Do-Good Foundation                  Organization Code: 005-2009-01

Project Name/Grant Purpose: Youth Leadership Council
Project/Program Director: Jane Smith, Vice President of Programs

Number of Clients to be Served: 320 youth aged 10–17 years
Program Sites: 12 sites (4 per semester)
Proposed Period: January 2008–December 2008

Activities:
- 8 week program with 30-minute sessions each
- 1 program per semester including summer
- Half-day youth conference in fall
- 5 community projects

Collaborators:
- Healthy Youth Inc. (for programs)
- City Hall (for conference)

Outcome Measurement: due January–February 2009
- 75% of youth will show increased leadership skills as tested through pre- and post-tests
- 90% of youth will indicate a high degree of satisfaction with the program
- 100% of collaborators will indicated a high degree of satisfaction with the partnership

Attachments:
- Original documents submitted to funder: budget, timeline of activities, collaborator MOUs
- List of Responsibilities and Deadlines

*I have read the above summary and associated grant award documents and agree to fulfill my responsibilities as specified.*

Signature: _____    Name: _____

Date: _____

Figure 9.1 *Sample Grant Summary*

should find out in advance whether some of the basic practices are followed, such as the creation of an organization code for each funding source in the finance system to track grant revenue and expenses. This helps to ensure a streamlining of the entire grant management function, including the use of line item expenses from the submitted and approved budget to book related expenses. Program staff should be aware of this code and should use it in all communications regarding the grant, including their own program records and files.

The finance department in conjunction with the grant management team should also formulate and explain the procedure for the approval and submission of expenses related to each specific grant. All staff members using grant funds should be required to submit formal notifications or requests for expense allocation to the finance department describing the reason for each expense and its grant-related category. The relevant line item from the submitted/approved budget should be recorded so that the expenses are tracked appropriately; a copy should be kept with the program staff and reviewed monthly in order to ensure that expenses do not exceed the budget. For capital projects or expenses over a certain amount, additional procedures may be implemented for purchase requisitions and submittal of multiple vendor quotes (see Figure 9.2).

Lastly, for proper compliance and reporting, it is essential to keep meticulous records of every aspect of the grant as well as the project, program, or campaign it is associated with. For a more formalized record maintenance structure, the organization may also create a centralized file folder for the grant to include all relevant information from the time of proposal submission to the end of the grant period. Many organizations prefer to keep proposal information separate from grant management systems; there is usually no problem with this method unless a clear lack of communication and cooperation exists across departments. Regardless, it is a good practice to retain all financial and programmatic records, supporting documents, evaluation data, and statistical information for a period of three years from the time of initial grant receipt.

| Funding Code | Expense | Amount | Line Item | Explanation |
|---|---|---|---|---|
| 005-2009-01 | Art supplies | $145.50 | Program supplies | Program supplies for Daycare Arts program |

Submitted By: _____ Date: _____

Approved By: _____ Date: _____

*Please attach all relevant receipts, travel logs, timesheets, vendor invoices, etc. Please make a copy for your records.*

Figure 9.2 *Sample Expense Allocation Form*

---

### Best Practice: Brazosport College

The Grant Administration Office of the Brazosport College in Lake Jackson, TX, has created a grant file checklist for each funded project. In addition to the contact information of key program people and the details of the grant, it specifies file categories that must be maintained by the program directors:
- Funder's rules and regulations
- Request for Proposal and/or Federal Register announcement (for government grants)
- Correspondence file
- Draft narrative
- Budget notes
- Program and staff notes
- Final narrative and full application
- Final budget and related forms
- Original contracts and award letters
- Timeline chart and logic/outcome chart
- Quarterly and annual reports
- Annual internal review notes and reports

Each grant-funded program has a complete centralized grant file maintained in the Grant Administration Office based on the records above. In addition to other advantages of this filing system, the most valuable benefit is that at the time of the annual audit, all relevant information for grant awards is present in a centralized location.

---

# Stewardship With a Difference

Generally speaking, the same stewardship principles used by fundraisers for individual donors can easily be applied to foundation donors as well. Many resources are available to learn about superior stewardship techniques including appropriate gift acknowledgment, ethical management and use of funds, frequent and targeted donor communications, and ongoing donor relations (1). Gift acknowledgment can take the form of a simple thank you letter, or a more elaborate expression of gratitude as used by Lutheran Social Services in Austin, TX. Wanting to appropriately thank a handsome grant by the Beaumont Foundation of America to buy new clothes for approximately 1,300 foster children, the agency requested foster families to take pictures of the children as they shopped and to collect thank you letters and drawings from them. The photographs, letters, and drawings were compiled into a 100-page scrapbook-type album and sent to the foundation as a thank you. According to feedback received from the foundation, the album is put out on the board table at each board meeting and board members receive immense pleasure by looking at the pictures and reading the letters.

Acknowledgment also takes the shape of public gift recognition through various means, such as press releases, newsletters, and annual reports. Because both corporate and private operating foundations are often enamored of this type of acknowledgment, nonprofits can use creative methods to ensure that grants are given the recognition they deserve. The Shea Center for Therapeutic Riding in Orange County, CA, began its 2007 annual report with a letter from its leadership saying "thank you" and then dedicated an entire page not to clients or donors, but to volunteers. On the other hand, the 2007 annual report of the YMCA of Greater Cincinnati was entitled Letters of Love, and in addition to the obvious—letters of appreciation written by clients—also used abbreviations such as LOL and XOXO to show love and happiness. Each page of the report had pictures, letters, or both; toward the end the financials were cleverly titled with another abbreviation: ROI.

Aside from the initial show of appreciation for a grant, organizations should also communicate with foundations throughout the year to update them on key program accomplishments and alert them to advances in the field. The concept of personalized donor stewardship reports can be utilized for some foundation funders as well by understanding the possible motivations behind each foundation grant and aligning these reports accordingly. They work especially well for family and corporate foundations, where it may be easier to establish a personal connection with trustees or volunteers. Needless to say, in addition to recipient letters and stories, these stewardship reports should include specifics about the program or project supported by the foundation. Grant professionals should discuss these reports with other fundraising staff to ensure that no overlap exists and to learn about stewardship plans already in place that may be expanded to include foundations. They may also need training or coaching on stewardship and donor relations from more experienced fundraising staff. Additional details about stewardship reports are given later in this chapter.

For foundation donors, care must be taken to fully understand their preference for ongoing communication—some prefer not to receive any further contact after the thank you letter, while others are receptive to multiple contacts throughout the year. It is therefore important to determine how many times during the year each foundation should be contacted for nonsoliciting communications; experts typically consider four times a year adequate and reasonable. The grant professional, together with the marketing and public relations staff, can consider ways to thank and keep in contact with institutional donors. Having in-depth knowledge of the needs, motivations, and preferences of foundation funders is essential so that no feathers are ruffled or eyebrows raised—sometime a fine line separates creative acknowledgment from excessive splurging of donor funds for promotional purposes. The marketing team by itself will typically not be in a position to know these donor preferences, and the grant professional can bring valuable information to the table as a result of prior research and personal expertise. Some of the discussion from Chapter 2 will also be helpful in formulating strategies in this regard.

Our research has found that respondents vary in the number of times per year they contact funders for nonsoliciting purposes: although a high number do so four or more times a year, some never communicate with current grantors (see Figure 9.3).

Nonprofits are also using a variety of creative communication methods designed specifically for foundations for ongoing nonsoliciting contact. A large majority of our respondents (73.1%) sent annual reports, newsletters, or brochures, but many also sent CEO letters, press clippings, and presentations throughout the year. Further, more than half (54.5%) communicated personally through phone calls to foundation officials (see Figure 9.4).

All the communication methods mentioned above are excellent techniques of donor relations as they relate to foundation funders. Just as Chapter 8

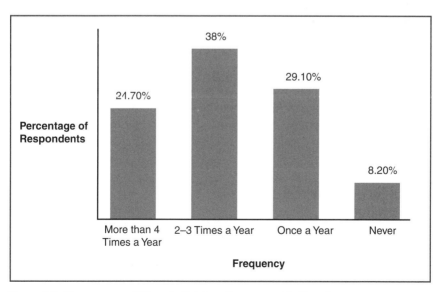

Figure 9.3 *Frequency of Non-Soliciting Contact with Funders*

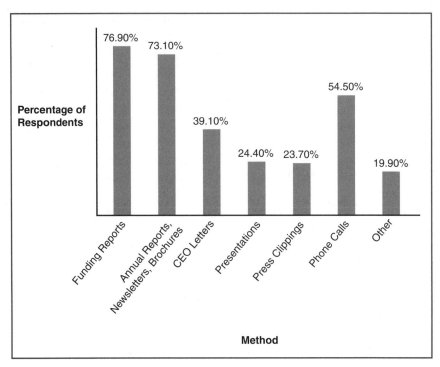

Figure 9.4 *Methods of Communicating with Funders*

details pre-grant site visits, postaward visits and events can also easily be held for foundation grantors as well, especially since they typically do not require a costly show such as individual donors may expect. Funders can also be invited to programmatic events and activities that are conducive to the presence of outsiders, *as long as no solicitation occurs.* Many foundation officials may refuse to attend nonprofit events, but some types of programmatic events—see Chapter 2 for explanations—can be of extreme interest to grantors and non-supporters alike.

# Reporting for Maximum Impact

The most common purpose of nonsoliciting contact, at least for institutional donors, is reporting back regarding the use of grant funds; as such, outcome reporting is a key aspect of any good foundation stewardship plan. Unfortunately, it often becomes a source of grief for grant professionals working in a noncooperative internal environment or for those in extensive facilities that make it difficult to communicate with key program staff and gather information in a timely manner.

Large foundations often have stringent reporting requirements that may place a heavy burden on the recipient organization. On the other hand, many small or family foundations have no specific reporting requirements at all, allowing recipients to forego reporting until and unless a new proposal is being submitted to them. Whether reports are mandatory or not, and regardless of whether any future funding is expected from a particular funding source, the fact remains that reporting should be understood as a self-evaluation and self-improvement tool for the organization itself. Nonprofits that take this stewardship activity seriously and report back to all funders regardless of requirements typically see benefits both internally and externally. As explained in Chapter 3, the process of collecting and gathering outcomes data and setting achievable targets has numerous advantages to the overall success of the organization and its programs; by discussing negative as well as positive results with funders, nonprofits can build trust and help funders learn more about important issues in the field. Also, the best time to create evaluation programs and outcome measurement plans is at the commencement of a new program; however, if a new grant is obtained, it signals an opportunity to re-examine the evaluation methods and determine if changes need to be made.

The grant professional should, either separately or within the grant management team, note the reporting requirements of the funding agency early in the grant period. Information such as the frequency of reports, the format and questions to be answered, and the outcomes to be measured will help in creating a reporting process that is painless and accurate. Periodic grant status meetings between the grant professional and program staff are essential not only for the sake of timely reporting but also to keep abreast of any challenges being faced in data collection or program activities. The sample Grant Summary Sheet (see Figure 9.1) presented earlier in this chapter can be used for this purpose, or another similar document with staff responsibilities can be created. A schedule for data collection and reminders should be established so that program staff is aware of when the reports are due and adequate time is created in their work schedule to ensure that tasks are completed. This schedule may be on a monthly, quarterly, or annual basis or any other timeline appropriate for the organization, such as a semester system or one month after every program evaluation.

Grant professionals are in a unique role to handle multiple reporting requirements and expectations, especially when different outcomes are required by different funders at varying times during the year, or in the case of national affiliates or United Way agencies that have very specific outcome requirements often not of interest to foundations. Therefore, at most organizations, the program staff should be responsible for measuring outcomes and implementing evaluation procedures, while the role of the grant professional role should be that of facilitator: reminding staff of reporting deadlines and requesting submittal of information when required. Which person or department writes the report can be determined based on the level of reporting necessary and the nature of questions asked by the funder—many foundations inquire about lessons learned in management which may be handled more adequately by the grants professional or development director, whereas program outcomes can be easily reported by front line program staff using print or electronic means.

Reporting may not seem like a creative task, but funder reports can be made interesting and informative if the foundation has less strict requirements or formats. While certain foundations provide a list of questions or even templates for program reports, others leave it up to the discretion of the grantee to determine the type and format of the information provided. Depending on the foundation and the grant amount—corporate foundations or small grant awards, for example—a one-page document with key program and organizational accomplishments, community collaborators, and funding partners should be sufficient. This type of report can also include some carefully selected client quotes and pictures and can be in color; the report can then be used throughout the year as a marketing or fundraising tool with key stakeholders and major gift donors.

Which information to capture for reports may be specified in the original grant proposal or the grant award; however, grant professionals and program staff can easily go beyond the basic requirements to report additional data that may be helpful in showing progress. For example, if the promised outcomes deal with the number of clients served, gathering additional data on race, income, and other demographic characteristics can prove very beneficial to the program. At the same time, funders who receive this data tend to view the applicant in a very positive light; they are also better equipped to understand the real needs of the organization's constituents and as a result may be more receptive to subsequent grant proposals.

Another method for improving reports is to create benchmarks or milestones that call for the capturing of data on a more frequent basis than the regular reporting cycle. For instance, even if the grant cycle is one year and clients are evaluated on an annual basis, intermediary targets every three months can easily be implemented and reported upon. Not only are these kinds of milestones welcomed by funders, but they can be tremendously beneficial for the purposes of tracking progress and making changes if necessary. As an example, if the grantee expects to serve 100 clients during the grant period, quarterly targets may be to serve at least 25 clients per quarter. This not only allows the organization to assess on a quarterly basis if their activities or processes are effective, but also offers an opportunity to contact funders and other stakeholders if targets are met or exceeded. If, in the above example, the agency serves 50 clients in the first quarter alone, a simple phone call or email to foundation officials with this proud achievement is bound to be very well-received.

Realizing the need to become more efficient and professional, some organizations have begun to implement corporate reporting and assessment tools to track and enhance their nonprofit operations. One such tool is the *dashboard*: just as the dashboard of a car allows the driver to check his current speed, fuel level, and engine temperature, the organizational dashboard allows staff and volunteers to monitor and measure progress of key indicators at a glance.

Dashboards may be in the form of charts or graphs, as shown below (Figure 9.5):

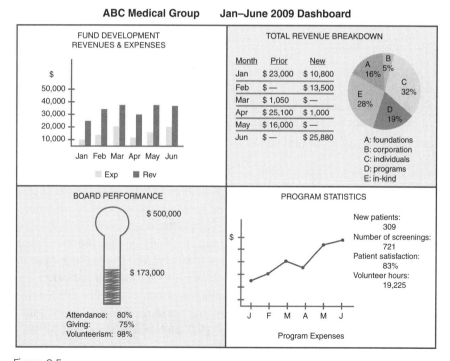

Figure 9.5

Dashboards may also be in the form of tables, as depicted in Figure 9.6:

**February 2009**

| Indicator | Feb 2009 Target | Feb 2009 Actual | Variance | Jan 2009 Actual |
|---|---|---|---|---|
| Revenues: | | | | |
| - Grants | $ 100,000 | $ 82,000 | ($ 18,000) | $ 50,500 |
| - Board giving | $ 25,000 | $ 18,150 | ($ 6,850) | $ 28,110 |
| - Number of new donors | 75 | 13 | (62) | 70 |
| - Number of new foundations, corporations | 10 | 12 | 2 | 17 |
| Programs: | | | | |
| - New volunteers recruited | 15 | 15 | 0 | 15 |
| - New clients enrolled: | | | | |
|   - ESL | 120 | 110 | (10) | 100 |
|   - Computer Competencies | 300 | 212 | (88) | 115 |
|   - Leadership workshops | 50 | 50 | 0 | 50 |
| Outcomes: | | | | |
| - Clients achieving learner gains | 75% | 80% | 5% | 77% |
| - Clients awarded certificates of completion | 50% | 42% | (8%) | 53% |
| - Dropout rate | 10% | 2% | 8% | 1% |
| Clients: | | | | |
| - Low income clients served | 90% | 96% | 6% | 82% |
| - Substance abusers served | 25% | 44% | 19% | 12% |
| - Children served | 50% | 23% | 27% | 20% |

Figure 9.6 *XYZ Agency Dashboard*

The Capital Area Food Bank in Washington, DC, uses a programs dashboard with quarterly and annual information for each of its programs in tabular form. For their Kids Café program, the dashboard measures the number of sites, the number of children enrolled, the number of meals served, the cost of the food, and the amount of food all captured per quarter and compared with the previous year. On the other hand, the Greater Chicago Food Depository has created a monthly dashboard with comprehensive organizational information including funding (total number of donors, gifts, foundation grants), staffing (number of staff and volunteers), and service information (total pounds distributed, total pounds received, and cost per pound). Their dashboard measures actual numbers with targets and keeps track of monthly variance for better performance measurement.

## Best Practice: Project Hope

A stakeholder is any person or entity with the potential of being affected by an organization's actions either directly or indirectly. In the corporate sector, strategic efforts focusing on both internal and external stakeholders are common, although nonprofits often tend to limit the extent of such activities to key constituents or to define stakeholders too narrowly. Project Hope, an international health organization based in Millwood, VA, understands the benefits of extending stewardship activities to all stakeholders; the organization creates "stakeholder reports" categorized according to major programs or issues such as infectious diseases, children's health, or humanitarian assistance. The reports are sent not only to current donors and funders, but to all those who have expressed an interest in a particular program or issue including potential funders who are working in a relevant field. The reports are comprehensive in nature and include updates, statistics, pictures, and human interest stories regarding the project or program in question. Rather than serving as fluffy marketing pieces, these reports contain detailed information regarding accomplishments and challenges, as well as explanations about internal and external processes, with the aim of keeping stakeholders informed and engaged. Each program, project, or issue area has its own stakeholder report; approximately two to three reports per year are sent in each category to a different set of stakeholders, although overlap may occur depending on interests of individuals or organizations.

Stewardship as a concept has its roots in medieval household management, whereby one person's property was managed by another. In the modern age, stewardship implies the considerate and conscientious use of environmental, financial, or other resources, keeping in mind the ideals of responsibility and accountability. As an extension, for the nonprofit organization, the stewardship of donors, including foundation donors, must necessarily involve ethical considerations as well. If changes to a funded project or program occur, funders should be informed immediately instead of waiting until the end of a grant period. Even if no reports are required, ethical practices dictate that these stakeholders be given accurate information regarding the use of their funds. Changes may be material in nature, such as a decline in clients served or a failure to measure outcomes as promised, or they may be other issues that the funder considers important and are mentioned in the proposal or reports, such as a change in key personnel or collaborators. Experience shows that in most cases, funders are sympathetic and understanding, as long as alternatives are discussed in a timely manner. The most considerate course of action is to inform a funder as soon as it becomes obvious that the activities or outcomes will not be achieved.

Another ethical consideration that may be more difficult to keep track of is the fiscal management of grant funds, especially if checks and balances are not created within the grant management plan or if finance and accounting staff do not form part of the grant management team. Transparency in the spending and recording of grant funds is one key aspect of good fiscal stewardship; another is the reporting and return of any grant funds left over at the end of the grant period. In many situations, the funder will allow the organization to utilize the funds either for another program or project or to carry over for the same purpose in the following grant period.

On the programs side, evaluation integrity and accuracy may be compromised either intentionally or mistakenly. The establishment of an ethics committee is one way to ensure that any unethical or illegal practices uncovered by a staff member are reported and resolved appropriately. Oftentimes, grant professionals may face resistance from program or organizational leaders who do not wish to inform funders about negative outcomes or failure to deliver promises. It then becomes the responsibility of the grant professional to continuously train and educate other staff members and volunteers about the importance of honesty and accountability for the sake of the organization's long-term interests.

Overall, nonprofit organizations can typically recover from past mistakes by maintaining honest and open communication lines with all stakeholders, including funders. Foundations realize that grant proposals are only plans that have been made with certain situations in mind, such as the current economic conditions or the internal capacities of the organization at a specific point in time. They are also aware that scenarios sometimes change dramatically and many external issues can arise that force the organization to deviate from its plan—this could be the resignation of a key staff member, the damage caused by a hurricane, or an unexpected breakdown of a key collaboration. It is only by trying to remain upfront and continuously seeking advice and understanding that the grantee–grantor relationship can be strengthened for the benefit of the nonprofit and the clients it serves.

## ENDNOTES

(1) See List of Suggested Resources.

# Chapter 9 Checklist

## Organizational Readiness

| Indicator | Status |
|---|---|
| Do we have post-award grants management policies and manuals in place for foundation grants? | |
| Do we have an interdepartmental grants management team for the purposes of checks and balances? | |
| Does program staff receive training on grants compliance and proper procedures to follow for spending and reporting grant funds? | |
| Does the finance department utilize formal methods for tracking grant revenues and allocating grant expenses? | |
| Are grants management records maintained in a central location for at least three years after awards have been made? | |
| Do we have a variety of donor-centric stewardship activities for foundations that ensure nonsolicitation? | |
| Is reporting considered a self-evaluation and self-improvement tool for the entire organization? | |
| Do our funder reports contain benchmarks and milestones? | |
| Do we utilize dashboards or other methods of reporting and assessment tools? | |
| Do we maintain ethical stewardship practices including informing donors of changes in funded programs or returning unused grant funds? | |

## Grant Professional Readiness

| Indicator | Status |
|---|---|
| Do I have a working knowledge of grants management regardless of whose responsibility it is in my organization? | |
| Have I created summary sheets or deliverables lists for all grants awarded? | |
| Am I aware of all procedures and documentation that program and accounting staff must follow for tracking, spending, and reporting grant funds? | |
| Do I keep records of all grant-related information including post-award management in one centralized location? | |
| Am I aware of individual funder preferences regarding gift acknowledgment and stewardship? | |
| Am I willing to learn from more experienced development staff about stewardship practices that can be implemented for foundation relations? | |
| Am I aware of each funder's reporting requirements, and have I communicated them in advance to all program and finance staff? | |
| Have I established a schedule for data collection and timely reporting that is understood and accepted by all program and finance staff? | |
| Do I regularly explain the importance of ethical grants management to my leadership and colleagues? | |

# Make Friends with Funders

*"As a foundation, we are acutely aware of power relationships. If you look at why [Liberty Hill was] created and how we have been working for the last three decades, it is apparent that we have been creating strategies for being more effective and leveling power inequalities. We have resources that nonprofits don't, and therefore our feeling is that the work they are doing in the community will be more effective if we work together as partners."*

Barbara Osborn, Director of Strategic Communications
Liberty Hill Foundation

By the time readers reach this last chapter, the concept of funders as friends should no longer be a surprising notion or a pipedream. The last but perhaps most important aspect of holistic grant seeking is to continually build relationships within the funding community regardless of whether any grants are awarded as a result. While it may not be cost effective for many organizations to pursue funders who are unlikely to ever financially support them, an argument exists to the contrary as well: when relationships are formed with foundations using strategic processes, funding will follow sooner or later as a result of the relationship rather than the grant proposal. On the other hand, making friends with grant makers can be time consuming, often requiring months or years of dedication on the part of an organization's senior leaders. The most successful of grantor–grantee partnerships can probably not be explained to or replicated by others. Despite the obstacles, however, most nonprofits can use simple and creative methods of relationship building by understanding the needs and interests of grant makers, and aligning themselves accordingly.

# Sustained Support

The best indication of an existing grantor's commitment and partnership is renewed funding over the years. Many new grant applicants complain that foundations form cliques with their long-time supporters, making it difficult for new organizations to obtain funding from them. Although at first glance this may seem true, especially for smaller or local foundations, the reason is compelling: if a grantee–grantor relationship is successful (outcomes are realized, clients are satisfactorily served, and a mutual community concern is addressed) the best option for a funder is to reinvest in an organization that has already shown results, rather than backing an unknown entity. Further, over the years personal and professional connections are also built between the staff and leaders of foundations and the nonprofits they support, leading to recurring grants.

Our research found that a majority (56.5%) of respondents received less than a quarter of their grants from foundations that had never supported them before (see Figure 10.1).

On the other hand, 39.1% of respondents received approximately 75% of all grant awards from previous funders, and 28% received half of all grant awards from funders who had supported them in the past (see Figure 10.2).

The good news for grant professionals is that this relatively straightforward form of grantee–grantor partnership can be established and maintained by conducting good grant management, reporting, and stewardship practices as described in Chapter 9. Just as existing individual donors are more receptive to subsequent donation requests, foundations that are currently supporting

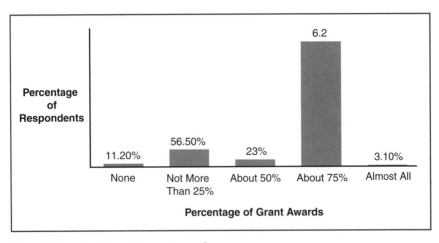

Figure 10.1 *First Time Grant Awards*

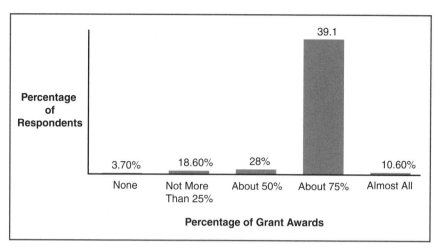

Figure 10.2 *Grant Awards from Previous Funders*

an organization, or had in the recent past supported it, will be the most amenable to subsequent grant proposals. The proposal process may be easier in these cases as well; for example, current grantees may be spared the initial round of proposal reviews or pre-proposal site visit or may have to submit fewer documents.

Some organizations have found that they have been funded by a family foundation for several years, sometimes even since their inception for no apparent reason. Rather than being a cause of celebration, however, this should give rise to questions and discussions in order to find out the cause of the long-term support; in some situations, it may be possible to increase the grant award just by implementing simple cultivation techniques borrowed from major gifts or annual fund departments. Prospect research can also be utilized to discover trends and possible connections with current grantors that may be unknown as a result of nonprofit staff turnover or lack of proper record keeping. See Chapter 6 for a detailed discussion of foundation prospect research.

From the foundation perspective, supporting current grantees in subsequent years has gained more popularity. The Triangle Community Foundation in Durham, NC, published a call to action in January 2009, which recommends that donors including institutional grant makers consider the strategic implications of their giving. In order to plan for the long-term, the report suggests that funders "consider the difference in impact of multiple small gifts or grants compared to sustained, deeper relationships with fewer nonprofit organizations" (1). Instead of building relationships, however, many organizations actually lose funding from past grantors for a variety of reasons. Although this may happen as a result of slowing economic conditions when foundations have fewer funds to give, many times a mistake on the part of the grantee leads to such a situation. Apart from issues of reporting or noncompliance with grant terms, other more personal factors such as a falling out among senior leadership may also play a role. Negative publicity or crisis may similarly affect a long-term funder's decision to reinvest in a particular organization. The advice offered in several chapters in this book can be helpful in dealing with the above-mentioned issues as organizations struggle to preserve grant awards over time.

Some foundations also have rules about continuous grant giving, preferring to terminate funding for a few years after three or more consecutive grant awards to the same nonprofit. In most cases, it is safe to assume that for a nonprofit organization, maintaining the status quo in terms of funding partners is helpful only for a few years, after which grant makers may begin to question the organization's lack of ability to attract other funding or to continue the program on its own. Although Chapter 7 explains how to deal with the issue of sustainability from a grant seeker's perspective, it is also important to remind grant professionals that many foundations are now beginning to ask serious questions about an organization's plan for self-reliance. By understanding that such a plan or strategy must come from senior staff and leaders, the grant professional can pave the way for initial discussions by bringing funder concerns to their attention and educating them on some ways to address these concerns.

Organizations can use many of the suggestions offered in previous chapters of this book to rejuvenate and revitalize relations with current and past funders in ways that will ensure continuous funding. For example:

- Encourage and motivate board members, senior staff, and volunteers to utilize their personal and professional connections with foundation officials, thereby enhancing the efforts of the grant professional (Chapters 1 and 6).
- Conduct external public relations activities that focus on the organization's positive contributions to the community and align with overall mission and brand (Chapter 2).
- Improve existing programs and services, enhance outcome measurement techniques, and conduct ongoing community assessment to evidence need (Chapter 3).
- Include collaborating agencies in the grant request and create new partnerships to serve more clients (Chapter 4).
- Invite current and past funders to site visits in order to highlight accomplishments and showcase results in an emotional setting (Chapter 8).
- Improve grant management techniques, conduct additional stewardship activities, and enhance the quality or number of reports to funders (Chapter 9).

On the other hand, support from foundations often takes the shape of nonmonetary assistance as well, although it takes a discerning nonprofit to truly understand and appreciate the long-term benefits of such practices. The Center for Effective Philanthropy recently published a report called "More Than Money: Making a Difference with Assistance beyond the Grant." The study reveals 14 different types of assistance offered by the foundation world to grantees in addition to the grant award itself, namely:

1. General management advice
2. Strategic planning advice
3. Financial planning/accounting
4. Development of performance measures
5. Encouraged/facilitated collaborations
6. Insight and advice on the field
7. Introductions to leaders in the field
8. Research or best practices
9. Seminars/forums/convenings
10. Board development/governance assistance
11. Information technology assistance
12. Communications/marketing/publicity assistance
13. Use of foundation facilities
14. Staff/management training (2)

Although the center's study is addressed to foundation officials trying to improve their social impact, nonprofits can also use the findings to encourage funders they are already familiar with to provide some of the assistance mentioned above, not only to their organizations but to the community in general. Care must be taken to match funder interest and capacity to the type of assistance being suggested; community foundations, for example, are more likely to offer technical workshops to nonprofits, while corporate foundations may be more interested in bringing agencies together for collaborating opportunities. Grant professionals who are aware of such practices can push for such nonmonetary support if relationships already exist with one or more grant maker.

# Peer Support

Seeking grants from existing funders may be the safest method of grant seeking, but organizations should also go a step further and use their supporters' leverage to acquire new grants. Just as individual fundraising techniques concentrate on peer giving by bringing in board members to make the "ask" to major gift prospects, new funders can be approached through peer encouragement from current funders, since the latter are already believers in the organization's mission and programs. If in doubt about the validity of such leverage, consider the fact that almost all foundation grant applications require a list of previous funders and grant amounts either within the grant proposal or as a separate document. Some foundations request such records from two or three years back as well, wanting to know which other local, regional, and even national foundations have been investing in the applicant over the long-term. Foundations are also very interested in who else within their peers is being solicited for the same request: our research discovered 16.5% of respondents reporting that "all" grant applications required a list of other foundations being solicited, and 37.3% saying that "almost all" required it (see Figure 10.3).

Peer support can take many forms, depending on the degree of commitment felt by the funder to either the organization, the issue it addresses, or the people (staff or board members) associated with it. Some foundation staff may make recommendations to their grantees about other funders interested in similar projects, allowing grant requests to become more targeted and personalized. Others may be willing to talk to their counterparts at similar foundations over the phone or in person or to submit letters of support on behalf of the grantee. Even foundations that reject a grant application may suggest alternative funders who may be more amenable to the application or program. Many grant makers (community foundations in particular) have options on their websites for donors to support their grantees; for example, the Eugene and Agnes E. Meyer Foundation in

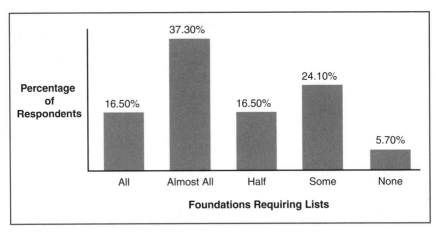

Figure 10.3 *List of Other Supporters Required*

Washington, DC, not only features grantees on their website but also offers readers the option to click on a "give now" button to donate to the charity being profiled. First and foremost, it remains the grant professional's duty to inquire about any such possibilities from foundation staff with whom relationships already exist on a staff level; board members and senior staff, and sometimes even program staff should be similarly encouraged during the grant seeking process to seek peer funding support using their personal and professional connections.

Consider Local Funding Partnerships (LFP), a national program of the Robert Wood Johnson Foundation, which personifies the power of leverage by granting funds to nonprofits based on the nominations of local funders. The aim of the foundation is to determine the degree of interest and commitment from funding partners, which is viewed as a key indication of local support for a proposed project. As part of the proposal process, the nominating funder writes the cover letter inviting LFP to join in a funding partnership, commits to providing matching funds, and agrees to organize other funders to contribute. Interestingly, LFP allows not only foundations to act as local funding partners, but almost all types of funding entities including United Way branches, corporations, local charities, and even fundraising revenue and individual benefactors. Although a relatively small number of organizations in the country are eligible to receive funds from LFP, grant professionals at any nonprofit can use this model to strengthen their applications to regional and national grant makers by harnessing the power of leverage. Even if a local foundation has not considered supporting an organization in this way, conversations between the senior leadership of both parties can give rise to a number of new possibilities.

In some situations, a nonprofit may not be in a position to seek peer support either due to internal limitations or because of a lack of relationships within the grant maker community in the region. Even if funders are generally unwilling or unable to lend their name or signature to any particular grant request on a nonprofit's behalf, it may still be possible to use their leverage to find new support. Public relations activities such as those mentioned in Chapter 2 can be used to publicize grant awards or other major support in order to reach potential grant makers who may be interested in joining the effort based on who else is involved. Smaller family foundations and corporate funders are most susceptible to this type of leverage, hence the more an organization reveals about grant sources and funded projects, the better. Potential supporters can be included in stewardship or program-related events to which current donors are invited and commended; in this way, newcomers not only learn more about the organization and its accomplishments, but also gain an opportunity to network with their peers in the field.

## Funder Perspective: Thrive by Five Washington
*Anne Baunach, Director of Fund Development*

Q: What is Thrive by Five Washington?

A: Thrive by Five Washington was born as a result of relationships within the philanthropic community, by funders and individuals who were interested in early childhood education. We are a unique public–private partnership created as a result of a state-wide agenda. In short, the state of Washington and the Bill and Melinda Gates Foundation came together to form Thrive. Even though we are a 501 (c) 3 nonprofit and raise money from the community to continue our efforts, we do not conduct any programs ourselves. We grant funds to other organizations that are working directly in the field and leverage our partnerships within the business and foundation community, for example through our board members, many of whom are representatives of area foundations, to support early learning initiatives in the state of Washington.

Q: Can you give an example of how Thrive by Five Washington leverages partnerships?

A: A year ago we created an Aligned Funding Initiative, a document that encouraged our peers to give substantial amounts of funds to one of our grantees. This initiative explained why we were investing in that organization, how it ties into our overall strategic plan, and the financial details such as the goal, our grant amount, and our request from our funding partners. Because of the recent economic downturn, we have put the initiative on hold, but that doesn't mean we are no longer involved with that organization. It just means that it may be a couple of years before we can resume the Aligned Funding Initiative itself. So in the meantime, we are conducting other activities to show our support and encourage our funding partners to give to the organizations and causes we consider important. We assist representatives of other foundations by guiding their giving practices and aligning themselves strategically within the state of Washington. We also look for organizations doing best practices in the state and recommend them to others who are looking to make grants. Encouragement and endorsement by Thrive can make a huge difference in other funders' decisions.

Q: What do you recommend for nonprofits wanting to approach new funders or build relationships with them?

A: For nonprofits, relationships are crucial because they can go back to their current or previous funders with whom they have had positive experiences in order to seek new support. While you have the funding, it is important to communicate regularly, do everything the proposal promised, and seek feedback from the funder, including suggestions for improvement. Even in tough economic times when funding capacity is diminished, relationships and partnerships with funders can be really helpful. If funders don't have money to invest in your organization, don't just disappear from their radar. Pull a foundation official onto a committee, for example. The more a foundation becomes engaged and involved in the work of the organization, the more it will continue the relationship when funds do become available.

# Funders as Partners

As mentioned in previous chapters, foundations depend on nonprofit organizations to solve community problems and make a desired social impact. However, the realities of power relationships are such that grant makers are considered to have the upper hand, while nonprofits are seen as beggars supplicating for funds. Many foundations prefer closed door policies, while others who establish communication lines with their grantees often do not level the playing field for non-grantee organizations aspiring to receiving support. Anecdotal evidence from our research also suggests that grant maker attitudes may differ based on their geographical location and whether they are located in urban or rural areas.

Fortunately, grant makers are becoming more and more aware of the value of partnering with the nonprofit community in order to serve the common good. As mentioned earlier in the chapter, many foundations offer field-related assistance to nonprofit organizations, including participation in roundtables, seminars, and forums, or through the dissemination of best practices and published research. Others offer their resources to the nonprofit community, such as free meeting space or technical assistance. Still other foundations bring nonprofit staff and leaders together for meetings or learning opportunities, such as the Liberty Hill Foundation in Santa Monica, CA, which holds three separate "peer roundtables" for executive directors, development staff, and community organizers, respectively. The purpose of these quarterly groups is for practitioners to share ideas and tools, network with each other, and seek guidance for pressing concerns.

Grant professionals should track the activities and events offered by local and regional funders that may be of value to their organizations, making an effort to attend not only for their technical benefit but also for networking purposes. For instance, the Triangle Community Foundation holds monthly events for nonprofit leaders called "Lunch with the President." The events are hosted by the foundation's president and include either a technical topic such as budgeting or fundraising, or are targeted towards specific groups such as new executive directors. For obvious reasons, meeting often with the president of a major local funder can reap benefits in the long run.

Going further, many grant makers actively seek input from nonprofits about community issues through focus groups, impact surveys, ad-hoc advisory committees, or specialized task forces; all these may be either convened for a specific purpose or time period or may constitute ongoing efforts forming the grant making process. Newly established foundations may invite organizations and community leaders to assist in identifying urgent community needs and to help establish grant making criteria and focus areas. Similarly, foundations serving large areas may establish local committees or councils; the El Pomar Foundation in Colorado Springs, CO, established nine regional councils to better understand and respond to the specific needs of local communities in 2003. As part of these councils, civic and nonprofit leaders joined by one El Pomar trustee per region, identify specific issues and needs in their regions and offer grant recommendations to the foundation. Also, certain types of foundations, such as health care conversion foundations, are required to create community advisory committees (CACs) in order to remain in-tune with health care issues in the community.

Many nonprofit executives feel that committing time or resources to participate in the above-mentioned activities is too costly in terms of time spent away from their nonprofit work. Such individuals should remember that gaining and keeping the attention of foundation staff can go a long way in building relationships that may translate into funding if they or their organizations are viewed as experts in the field. Additionally, even though such opportunities to serve may be few, nonprofits can also take the initiative in encouraging local funders to partner with them in various ways, such as by bringing organizational or community needs and challenges to their attention. A trend towards grantee perception reports prove that funders are open to nonprofit suggestions and are increasingly looking to their counterparts in the field to explain the challenges they are facing on a day to day basis. In particular, smaller foundations may not be aware of critical issues until they are brought to light by practitioners, after which they may be more than willing to provide solutions in terms of technical or financial support.

Several examples exist of nonprofit–funder partnerships for the benefit of the community or field as a whole. Nonprofits may partner with like-minded funders to convene conferences, conduct needs assessments, or publish reports. They may also bring new service delivery models or outcome management techniques to funders' consideration. Regardless

# Funder Perspective: Foundation for a Healthy Kentucky
*Mary Jo Dike, Program Manager*

Q: How can nonprofits partner with funders in the community?

A: There are often opportunities for nonprofits to serve on committees or events that a foundation may be sponsoring, for example, our annual forum on health policy convenes every fall is a good way to get engaged with us through participation or by volunteering to help with planning. We talk with our board members and advisory board to find people for the planning committee. Regardless of whether a funder is involved or not, finding collaborations or coalitions to serve on helps nonprofit leaders become aware of issues in the community whether by engaging in their own networks or outside their networks. An example might be a group of interested nonprofits serving the uninsured. We as a funder keep an eye on what these groups are doing because we try to pay attention to what's going on in the community. So serving on these committees or networks can be beneficial to them; it doesn't mean they get to bypass a funder's application process, but by being out in the community and engaged in the larger issues they raise their visibility.

Q: How does your foundation involve nonprofit practitioners and community leaders?

A: Our CAC is a 31-person committee nominated and elected from the community. The criteria for selection are very diverse in terms of nonprofits they represent, as well as ethnic and gender diversification. The CAC is an extension of our board of directors; although it does not have fiscal or policy responsibility, it liaisons with the community and keeps issues in the forefront. The CAC provides input and guidance to the board of directors on the climate and advises how to proceed. In addition, the CAC has a lot of power because it is responsible for appointing the majority of foundation board members; in fact, from time to time a CAC member may go on to sit on the foundation board. The CAC includes a wide array of community members from doctors and nurses to retired engineers, politicians, health educators, and outreach coordinators of local hospitals. The relationship between the foundation board and the CAC is healthy; the board sees the CAC as a resource to help it do its job better, and CAC members also sit on board committees to offer their expertise. CAC membership itself has enormous benefits: the opportunity to engage with other experts on health issues, the ability to network and build connections, and the opportunity to provide input on how funding resources are dispensed. Nonprofit leaders who recognize the value of this commitment also reap the benefits in the long run.

of the type of collaboration, it is important to remember that discussing partnership possibilities with grant makers is not an easy task; it requires some sort of past relationship in terms of board or staff connections or prior funding, or an expression of interest by the grant maker through a Request for Proposal or other means. Grant professionals can assist in this initial process by fully grasping the issues faced by the program staff as well as by the entire field in which the organization works; for example, for a nonprofit working in healthcare, program staff may be repeatedly seeing uninsured clients with dental problems or there may be a general understanding that no local dental programs exist to serve uninsured residents of a certain community. Grant professionals who are involved in program design, implementation, and operations, as explained in Chapters 3 and 4, will remain fully aware of challenges faced by staff (not being able to serve patients adequately because of a lack of dental services) and the community at large (deteriorating dental health of low income families); by keeping track of the interests and capacity of local foundations as discussed in Chapter 6, they will also know exactly which foundation official can be approached with suggestions of a new dental health initiative. Some questions to ask as the process is formalized are given below.

1. Is this a genuine need for the community or my organization? What information has been gathered to assess the need—who has been consulted and what documentation has occurred?

2. What are some possible solutions to the problem being addressed? Are the solutions creative, feasible, and sustainable? What are the costs associated with each solution?

3. What is the process for selecting the best solution?

4. Who can be approached to assist in implementing the solution both programmatically and financially? How can the interest and capability of each possible partner be assessed? Do any relationships already exist with potential partners?

5. What is the best plan of action for approaching potential partners? Who within the organization or its stakeholders can participate in this process?

Finally, collaborating with the foundation community can seem daunting, especially if local grant makers are resistant to open communication. The best method of building long-lasting relationships with current and future grantors is to follow the counsel offered in this book, making sure that internal processes are improved, external partnerships are cemented, and grant management becomes rewarding rather than cumbersome. As a result, this last step of the cycle of holistic grant seeking will also become the first step, as nonprofit leaders who take the findings and recommendations of this book to heart get ready to come full circle.

## ENDNOTES

(1) Triangle Community Foundation Triangle Gives Back: A Call to Action, January 2009. www.trianglegivesback.org/elements/media/files/TGB_Call_to_Action_-_Final.pdf

(2) More than Money: Making a Difference with Assistance beyond the Grant: The Center for Effective Philanthropy. Buteau E, Buchanan P, Bolanos C, Brock A, Chang K. More than Money: Making A Difference With Assistance Beyond the Grant. Center for Effective Philanthropy 2008. www.effectivephilanthropy.org/images/pdfs/CEP_More_than_Money.pdf

# Chapter 10 Checklist

## Organizational Readiness

| Indicator | Status |
|---|---|
| Do we have good relationships on an institutional level with funders that currently support us? | |
| Have we maintained good relationships on an institutional level with funders that have supported us in the past? | |
| Have we addressed any concerns of current or past funders that may present obstacles to future funding? | |
| Do our staff and board understand and utilize the value of leverage when seeking grants from a variety of sources? | |
| Is each employee and volunteer of our organization encouraged and trained to identify, establish, and build relationships with funders in the community? | |
| Do we publicize grant awards adequately through public relations activities? | |
| Do we participate in activities offered by local grant makers for the benefit of the nonprofit sector? | |
| Do we actively seek and engage in nonprofit–funder partnerships? | |

# Grant Professional Readiness

| Indicator | Status |
|---|---|
| Do I bring funder concerns to my leadership for the purposes of establishing and improving current relationships and future grant seeking efforts? | |
| Am I aware of nonmonetary assistance from the grant making community that may be available to my organization? | |
| Do I make current funders aware of peer gifts through my conversations or in my proposals? | |
| Do I seek regular feedback from funders about my proposals and our programs? | |
| Do I inform my leadership and program staff of opportunities to work with grant makers in the community? | |
| Do I encourage my leadership to suggest ways of overall improvements in the field that can be communicated to grant makers? | |

# The Future of Grant Seeking

"We give a lot of attention to strategic planning. If we give a grant to an organization, can they sustain the programs? Do they have a board that is committed to their services? Have they looked at themselves strategically?"

W. Joseph Mann, Director of Rural Church Programs
The Duke Endowment

rant professionals may wonder after reading this book if they have been charged with changing the world single-handedly. In some organizations, especially where old-school values and rigid attitudes flourish, that may certainly seem the case. The qualitative results of our research indicate that nonprofits are focused on grants often to the exclusion of other, more creative fundraising techniques. This is more often the case with smaller organizations without fundraising staff to support more intensive development efforts like donor relations, annual funds, planned giving, and major gifts.

There are many reasons for this fascination with grant writing. For one, the "cold proposal" method often presents cost savings to nonprofits already strapped for cash. Secondly, applying for, and receiving, a large grant can be less time consuming and more rewarding than making continuous efforts to find and connect with donors both individual and institutional. Such short-term thinking is useful in situations where the immediate goal of paying the current year's bills is more important than the long-term gains in relationship building or community rebranding recommended in this book.

But grant professionals should remain very optimistic about the future of grant seeking in their own organizations as well as the industry in general. The research-backed advice provided here should not be considered a herculean task that needs years of effort or vast amounts of resources to accomplish. All the best practices and funder recommendations provided in this book can be implemented with few actual costs and often little resistance from staff and volunteers. Even the practices of billion-dollar institutions can be translated into creative yet small improvements more applicable to smaller nonprofits.

Although our investigation of factors affecting foundation giving and the subsequent interviews and best practice discussions occurred in better economic times, the results of the research become even more relevant during economic downturns. Nonprofit organizations are finding themselves relying on foundation grants more than ever before, whereas foundations are themselves feeling the pinch of reduced endowments and investments. Many corporate funders have all but halted charitable giving and community foundations are competing with area nonprofits for individual donors who no longer have the capacity to give. Is there hope for an ordinary 501 (c) 3? Not for those that use a hit-or-miss approach to submit standard grant proposals to every foundation listed in the local funder directory. But organizations that understand the value of building relationships and creating a positive image in the community will remain unfazed because these activities now become even more important than before.

Grant seeking in any type of environment is challenging, so grant professionals may need to take the initiative to inform and educate their colleagues, peers, and seniors about creative and sustainable changes they can all make in their external and internal environments. Using the information in this book, an overhaul can occur in the community as a result of long-term strategies. Some recommendations from our research become extremely pertinent when applied to situations in which organizations struggle with limited resources and community needs grow rapidly. For example, efforts to motivate and energize board members, conduct strategic planning and mission reassessment, and collaborate with similar nonprofits and funders in areas of mutual concern all cost relatively little but can reap huge benefits over the years. As foundations realign their focus and priorities and prefer to give to organizations they are familiar with, organizations working towards relationships through superior research, board member connections, and high-quality stewardship stand to gain.

The proposal writing process itself can be adapted to make more sense of the present world as well. Narratives should center on heightened community problems, more recent needs assessments, or outcomes that are likely to be lost if funding is abandoned. Teamwork and cooperation between program, marketing, and grants departments is even more crucial in providing the most appropriate information to funders and remaining flexible in program design and development. Stewardship practices can be enhanced and adapted to inform key stakeholders about the positive changes an organization is making to assist their street, neighborhood, city or state.

Funders and nonprofits alike are facing a tough world going forward. The need of the hour is a grant seeking strategy that goes beyond the proposal itself and involve the entire organization from the top down. Grant professionals who take the first step will indeed benefit themselves, their organizations, and their communities in a very positive manner. We wish our readers the best of luck as they apply the research and funder advice to their grant seeking efforts.

# LIST OF SUGGESTED RESOURCES
## Board Development and Fundraising

BoardSource. The Nonprofit Board Answer Book: A Practical Guide for Board Members and Chief Executives. Hoboken, NJ: Jossey-Bass, 2007.

Burk P. Donor Centered Fundraising. Montreal, Quebec: Burk & Associates Ltd., 2003.

Duca DJ. Nonprofit Boards: Roles, Responsibilities and Performance. Hoboken, NJ: Wiley, 1996.

Lansdowne D. Fundraising Realities Every Board Member Must Face. Medfield, MA: Emerson & Church, 2008.

Schaff T, Schaff D. The Fundraising Planner: A Working Model for Raising the Dollars You Need. Hoboken, NJ: Jossey-Bass, 1999.

Zimmerman RM, Lehman AW. Boards That Love Fundraising: A How-To Guide for Your Board. Hoboken, NJ: Jossey-Bass, 2004.

## Public Relations

Beckwith SJ. Publicity for Nonprofits: Generating Media Exposure that Leads to Awareness, Growth, and Contributions. New York: Kaplan Business, 2006.

Bonk K, Griggs H, Tynes E. Strategic Communications for Nonprofits: A Step-by-Step Guide to Working with the Media to Generate Publicity, Enhance Fundraising, Build Membership, Change Public Policy, Handle Crises, and More! Hoboken, NJ: Jossey-Bass, 1999.

Feinglass A. The Public Relations Handbook for Nonprofits: A Comprehensive and Practical Guide. Hoboken, NJ: Jossey-Bass, 2005.

## Strategic and Business Planning

Allison M, Kaye J. Strategic Planning for Nonprofit Organizations: A Practical Guide and Workbook. Hoboken, NJ: Wiley, 1997.

Horan JT, Jr. The One-Page Business Plan for Nonprofit Organizations. Berkeley, CA: The One Page Business Plan Company, 2007.

Jackson PM. Nonprofit Strategic Planning: Leveraging Sarbanes-Oxley Best Practices. Hoboken, NJ: Wiley, 2007.

Tiffany P, Peterson SD. Business Plans for Dummies. Hoboken NJ: For Dummies, 2004.

## Program Design and Evaluation

Linden RM. Working Across Boundaries: Making Collaborations Work in Government and Nonprofit Organizations. Hoboken, NJ: Jossey-Bass, 2002.

McNamara C. Field Guide to Nonprofit Design, Marketing and Evaluation. Minneapolis, MN: Authenticity Consulting, LLC, 2006.

Pawlak EJ, Vintner RD. Designing and Planning Programs for Nonprofit and Government Organizations. Hoboken, NJ: Jossey-Bass, 2009.

Peter F. Drucker Foundation for Nonprofit Management. Meeting the Collaboration Challenge Workbook. Hoboken, NJ: Jossey-Bass, 2002.

Taylor-Powell E, Rossing B, Geran J. Evaluating Collaboratives: Reaching the Potential. Madison, WI: University of Wisconsin Extension, 1998.

Wholey JS, Hatry HP, Newcomer KE. Handbook of Practical Program Evaluation. Hoboken, NJ: Jossey-Bass, 2004.

## Prospect Research

Birkholz JM. Fundraising Analytics: Using Data to Guide Strategy. Hoboken, NJ: Wiley, 2008.

Hogan C. Prospect Research: A Primer for Growing Nonprofits. Sudbury, MA: Jones & Bartlett, 2007.

## Grant Writing

Browning BA. Grant Writing for Dummies. Hoboken NJ: For Dummies, 2008.

Hall MS, Howlett S. Getting Funded: the Complete Guide to Writing Grant Proposals. Portland, OR: Continuing Education Press, 2003.

Quick JA, New CC. Grant Seeker's Budget Toolkit. Hoboken, NJ: Wiley, 2001.

## Grant Management

Quick JA, New CC. Grant Winner's Toolkit: Project Management and Evaluation. Hoboken, NJ: Wiley, 2000.

Ward D. Effective Grants Management. Sudbury, MA: Jones & Bartlett, 2009.

# Index